I SURVIVED

by

Ericka Bailey

To Sister Ethel,

Our God is
great and greatly
to be praised
Because of His
goodness. We
survived!
Rev.
Ericka

All scripture quotations were taken from the New Revised Standard Version (NRSV), the New International Version (NIV), the New Living Translation (NLT), and the King James Version (KJV).

For Copies Contact: Ericka@ISurvivedMinistries.org

For booking inquiries: ErickaBailey15@gmail.com

www.ISurvivedMinistries.org

Cover and Interior Design: Lauren Johnson/Pink Dragon Design

Printed and Bound in the United States of America

ISBN 978-0-692-86293-3

I dedicate this book to my fellow survivors, those of you who have carried the secret shame of physical, sexual and emotional abuse for far too long. Please know that I stand with you boldly declaring we have remained silent long enough. I encourage you to join me in the pledge to end the silence by advocating for yourselves and others who have suffered at the hand of their perpetrators. You my sister, my brother, are fearfully and wonderfully made and deserve all that God has in store for you. You are beautiful, strong and mighty. You Survived for a reason so rise up and make your presence known in the world.

I love you and thank you for resilience, strength and courage. You are a true Survivor!

– Ericka

"To all who mourn in Zion, he will give a crown of beauty for ashes, a joyous blessing instead of mourning, festive praise instead of despair. In their righteousness, they will be like great oaks that the LORD has planted for his own glory"

— Isaiah 61:3 —

Contents

I SURVIVED

Prologue

This is My Story

will admit, I was too young to remember any of this but by all accounts, the old, dilapidated South Side apartment reeked of alcohol and musty, stale cigarettes. My father laid passed out in a drunken stupor. My mother, broken and battered, yet determined, eyed my father carefully. It was imperative that she plan her escape just right. It was a matter of life and death. With six one dollar bills to her name and another three dollars in change, she roused my sisters and me from our sleep, loaded us in the car and began our less than fantastic voyage from Chicago to Quincy, IL, the place I would call home. Unfortunately, the further south we traveled on I-55, the more difficult my breathing had become. Eventually she would have to detour to a small, remote hospital where I was to receive an official diagnosis of asthma, two injections, and a prescription for medication that mom had no idea where she would find the money to fill.

Cast down but not destroyed, she resumed her journey, traveling as far as she could go until her luck and gas ran out, leaving her no choice but to reach out to an older brother, Charles Lee, who without hesitation traveled the highway to pick us up, stripped our old Oldsmobile of anything with a modicum of value and whisked us safely to the waiting arms of Quincy.

1

Life Without Dad

may be grossly underestimating, but according to
my memory, I can count on one hand—okay maybe two hands, the number of encounters I have had
with my father. This lack of relationship with him has
left a void in my life that has taken years to resolve. I
very much wanted and needed a daddy. Throughout
my childhood, songs like "Daddy's Home to Stay"
used to tear me up. And nobody knew. Who do you
tell? Who can you talk to? You don't. You just keep
rolling with the punches, keep on going, keep playing with other kids, keep growing up, keep going to

school, acting as if everything is fine.

Back in the 70's, a song used to come on the radio that included these lyrics. "I heard my momma cry. I heard her pray the night Chicago died." I was four or five years old at the time. That song messed me up. I was traumatized every time it came on the radio. I reasoned that if Chicago died, then my dad died too and with it went my dreams of ever knowing him. That is the only thing that made sense. Perhaps a part of me wanted to believe it because otherwise, why would a father not long to have a relationship with his own flesh and blood. Did he forget he had a daughter? I wanted to know him. Surely, he would want to know me as well. He had to be dead! That was the only thing that made sense, right? I wanted to accept that truth because the alternative meant that he simply was not interested in knowing me. Sadly, I could not figure out what I had done to make my father not want to know me. It broke my heart then. It breaks my heart today. I have always longed to be a daddy's girl.

2

Growing Up

My mother's name is Royce, she is affectionately known as "Rolls Royce" and while I have little problem typing her name, you would be hard pressed to hear me "say" her name. This is because our mother was revered in our household. My mother meant what she said and she said what she meant. We grew up during a time that parents disciplined their children and back then, whoopings were legal. Mom believed what the Bible said, "if you spare the rod, you spoil the child." Our roles were clear; she was the mother and we were her children. She was both mother and father in our household and recognized that statistically speaking, she was outnumbered by a ratio of four to one. But we weren't fooled for though she was small in stature, we knew that momma didn't take no mess. Mom mastered the art of non-verbal communication and one side-look was all it took to get all four of us into quick formation.

Mom was a hard worker and always worked outside of the home, so while we were getting ready for school, she was getting ready for work. I would dress as quickly as I could so that I could watch as she applied the finishing touches to her make-up, completed the final rotation with her curling iron, applied a dab of perfume to her delicate wrists as well as behind both ears. In my world, a more beautiful woman simply did not exist and I was enamored by her exquisite beauty. She was as delicate as a flower while simultaneously being as tough as nails as she braved the hand that life had dealt her. Her responsibilities were many and I watched her as she rose each day, unwilling to break, refusing to throw in the towel but determined to try again another day for her sake and for the sake of those she brought into the world. Mom is quite a woman and I like to think I get my strength from her. I used to wrap my little body around the bottom of her leg and hold on as she walked just to stay attached to her as she moved throughout the house. Eventually she would tire out and gently shake me off. Then I would break into song loudly singing Air Supply's "You're Every Woman in the World to Me!" I adored my beautiful momma.

I also have three older sisters; Charroy, Genel, and Adrian. Charroy is the oldest and she inherited much of the culinary skills in the family. It's not that the rest of us can't cook but Charroy can throw down! I'm not quite sure how that happened; were cooking classes offered at home in the beginning and later discontinued? Charroy can cook and the rest of us, well, we get by. Charroy was also in the Drum and Bugle Corps so some of our time was spent watching her perform with her troops. She was good, kept those knees marching high, face to the front, somehow managing to block out the squeals of delight from her younger sisters screaming her name from the sidelines. Charroy maneuvered that rifle and performance flag with great skill and a confidence second to none. Mom stood with us, beaming with pride as Charroy marched along following the drum major's orders, "Left, left, left-right left!" On and on she marched.

Charroy is eight years older than I am and it is natural that some older sisters don't want to be bothered with their younger siblings. Charroy wasn't like that. She made time for us, inviting us into her world, whether it was simply watching TV or letting us listen to some of the latest albums she purchased. Back then everything came either on a 78 or 45 size vinyl record. She had everything from Switch, Motown, Peaches and Herb, Kool & the Gang, The O'Jays to Sly & the Family Stone. The world was our stage.

When Charroy moved out and got her own apartment, I spent many nights bunking out on her

couch. I enjoyed staying with her and being the re-
cipient of the love and affection she showed me.

My sister Genel is second to the oldest. She is
three years older than I am. I would have to say that
she inherited the rhythm in the family. Genel could
dance! Her children would probably dispute this fact
but Genel could get down. I can see her now danc-
ing to Michael Jackson's "Shake Your Body Down to
the Ground!" Get it Nel! Those were the days. Not
wanting to age myself or her, but I remember when
music videos were in their inception, back in the day
of VH1, Genel could look at the videos and learn the
moves in 2.2 seconds. It would take me more like 2.2
months. By the time I learned the dance moves, the
dance was out of style. Genel was also into theater
and performed with my mother in a number of pro-
ductions at Quincy Community Little Theater.

Genel was fiercely protective of her sisters. She
stood a head and feet taller than most of the kids in
our neighborhood and would step in at the drop of
a hat if one of them were picking on her baby sisters.

She didn't mind "getting you" herself. I think she considered it her job to do so. I believe she thought she was our second mother but she would double dog dare one of the other kids to try to fight us. She loved us and while she wanted to rule the roost, she has always had our best interest at heart. Genel is a very loyal person and will give her last to help those who are in need.

My sister Adrian is born one year and one day before me. Her birthday is March 1st and mine is March 2nd. Isn't that just too amazing! This has always been too awesome to me. Mom says that I have always tried to follow in her footsteps and do everything that she does because of this and perhaps she is right.

Now, let me preface this next statement so I don't get myself in trouble here. All of us in the family are reasonably intelligent, okay? But I must say that my sister Adrian inherited the brains. She is a Brainiac. See, what I mean, is that even a word? I received a good education in the public-school system but Adrian was my math tutor from the 5th grade through… well, last week. Whenever I have a question about something remotely related to a mathematical equation, I call Adrian. I could not have made it without her. For me, the concept of math was lost in translation. She had a way of explaining it well enough that it somehow began to make sense. She was patient and kind and never made me feel "less than" for not getting it. Even now I am wondering if the less than sign goes < or >. Adrian, where are you???

I have wonderful sisters and share great memories of us putting bath towels on our heads as wigs, pretending to be Diana Ross or Natalie Cole singing their latest tunes. I always claimed it was "my turn" first and they usually gave in lest I collapsed in a crying fit. They loved their baby sister and it bothered them to see me upset.

My sisters would often go to bat for me, being willing to cover for my many shenanigans. Oftentimes I would get punished by being banned from watching TV and inevitably one of my sisters would

either try to take the blame or beg mom for my re-
prieve. When their efforts failed, they would take
turns sitting in the room with me so I would not have
to be alone while everyone else was having fun without me. I guess some would say I was a little spoiled.
I thank God for the love of my sisters.

3

Ever Changing Times

t was Charles Dickens who said "It was the best of times, it was the worst of times…" Of that, I could certainly relate. We grew up in the projects. Now granted, the projects of Quincy were vastly different than the projects of Chicago but they were the projects nonetheless.

Mom worked every day to keep food on our table and clothes on our backs. Despite all her efforts, we grew up "financially challenged" but we really did not feel inferior because many of our neighbors shared the same plight. There was a sense of community and it felt good to be as the "Cheers" theme song suggests, "where everybody knows your name."

It was great living in close proximity to so many of our family and friends. Much of our time was spent playing outside or hanging out at the local community hall, which we affectionately called "the center." The center was a recreational building that was owned by the housing authority. The center offered a safe place for children to congregate while providing productive activities that allowed us to learn and grow. We played board games, listened to music, participated in exercise classes, played foosball and ping pong, checked out books from the book mobile, danced, sang, ate. They even had a real live pin-ball machine. I loved going to the center.

The center is where I learned the music of Dionne Warwick and Phyllis Hyman. I played their music repeatedly. I would take my stage on top of a desk, grabbing the nearest pen or pencil to use as my microphone and sing, sing, sing. Poor Cornell Benford, who worked there at the time, had quite a time forcing me to comply with the rules. Those were the days.

I also recall getting dolled up just to go walking around the block in Quincy. It wasn't just any block. It was the city block that covered the perimeter of the projects. I know it sounds strange but so much went down in the projects. It was a hub of constant activity. The basketball court was always packed with the brothers playing ball. In the baseball field, there was often a baseball or softball game going on. The side of the field was lined with concrete benches where my friends and I would often stop and offer up a few impromptu cheers. "My back is aching, my bra's too tight. My booty's shaking from the left to the right. So, when you see me coming around, shake your body on to the ground!" We thought we were doing something.

On a good day, you could catch a good fight or two in the field. You could be walking around minding your own business or inside the center listening to music. Somehow, someway, word would get out that there was a fight going down in the field, and everybody would drop what they were doing and off we would go to root during the playground brawl. Those were the days when a fight was just a fight. You fought and it was over. We knew nothing about the use of guns and drive-by retaliations. It was a different day and time.

I had my share of friends back then, but I wasn't exactly a part of the in crowd. I looked up to the older girls in the neighborhood who were cute, popular and wore nice clothes. I saw things in them that I admired and tried to emulate them but I couldn't quite pull it off. I remember when the jheri curl came out—everybody was getting one. The jheri curl had the power to change black hair from being rough and difficult to manage, to hair that was soft, shiny and curly. I begged and pleaded with my mom to get me a curl. She finally relented and I was thrilled. I just knew this would boost my popularity rating. However, something went horribly wrong with the process (pun intended). For some reason, my jheri curl would not hold moisture. After I had gotten my hair done, my friends wanted to go walk around the block as we often did. I agreed to do so but because my curl kept drying out, I had to keep running in the house to douse my hair with water and then come back outside to resume my walk. And before you ask, I used the curl activator too. For some reason, it didn't work. I felt like the twins on the Super Friends cartoon. "Wonder-twin powers, activate! Shape of a comb, form of a pick!" I tried any and everything to get my curl to act right. It never did and I ended up going back to the standard wash and press. There went my hopes of joining the cool club.

But all in all, I felt loved and accepted with the girls in my fairy tale of mutual co-existence until the day our friend's house caught on fire. This "friend" lived a couple of blocks away in a house, a real house with a white picket fence. She had a momma and a daddy. She even had a dog too.

Our family along with several others pitched in to donate household items and clothing for this family who had lost everything. We went through each item carefully selecting which of our shirts and pants to give away. It took a while for the family to get back on their feet but eventually they did.

After about a week of absence from class, my friend returned to school. I, along with the rest of the students, was happy to see her return until I heard what she was going around saying about my family. She told everyone who would listen that her mom threw out everything that we had given to them. Her mother said neither she nor her younger sister would ever wear clothes donated by our family—as though we were not good enough. She then put us on blast by announcing that our house was full of roaches and that we had given them roaches when we brought our things over. For the record, everybody who lived in the projects had roaches. It's not as if we brought them to the projects. They were there before we got there. They were a part of the welcome committee when we moved in. When we tried to get rid of them, they didn't die, they multiplied. They were just a part of living in the projects. My friend's family should have known that they needed to shake the items out real good. That was on them. But, I digress.

I was humiliated and needless to say, I had to defend our household and the fight was on! This was the first of many childhood fights. I would fight at the drop of a hat. Truth be told, I've never been able to fight but I talked a big game and would "windmill fight" somebody to death. In case you are not familiar with the "windmill fight," it's when you ball up your fist, close your eyes, and go all in swinging wildly towards your opponent hoping and praying that one of your random punches will somehow make contact. If my opponent happened to grab hold of me, I would cat-scratch 'em to death! As such, I got a reputation of being a tough girl, a real fighter, and I wore that badge with pride.

I had also started to develop the art of taking things that did not belong to me; you know, the old five finger discount...Stealing! If I wanted something, I took it. I started off by stealing from the cold lunch

4

Getting to the Truth

became a problem child very quickly. Family members, church members, teachers, and principals saw the symptoms but they missed the root cause of my self-destruction. They missed the red flags. Something was wrong. I was being eaten alive but I did not know how to save myself. Though I had caring adults around me, I couldn't find the words to describe what I was going through and my silent screams went unanswered.

So, I acted out. I used fighting as a way of dealing with my emotional pain. Fighting was a way for me to release the feelings of powerlessness, the pent-up frustrations of hurt and shame that I carried within me each and every day. I did not have the words to say that someone was hurting me, doing things to me that they should not be doing. I could not find the words.

I was five years old when the sexual abuse started. Mom had a long-time sister friend who I will call "Ms. D." who came to visit from time to time. Mom worked hard during the week, leaving for work early each morning and coming home each evening to handle her responsibilities. We were excited when her girlfriends came to call as this gave us a chance to see mom in a different light. For just a little while, she was released from her primary role of single parent and got to step into the role of friend. Oh, they would talk and laugh, share the latest gossip. It was nice to see mom just "be." Sometimes, I would sit as still as possible to not get noticed so that I could soak up all the grown-up gossip. They would talk on and on until they finally noticed that nosy little Nikkie was still in the room.

One day Ms. D arrived with a man she intro-
duced as her husband. From that point on, every time
she came to visit, her husband would accompany her.
The visits between mom and Ms. D weren't quite the
same. They seemed somehow more subdued. My sisters and I grew restless after a while during their visit
and Ms. D's husband volunteered to take my sisters
and me to the park. Like all kids, we were thrilled to
go. When we got there, we eagerly jumped out of the
car and away we would go. We would run, jump and
scream and have the time of our lives. I remember it
like it was yesterday. I was allowed to play for a few
minutes before Ms. D's husband would call me back
to the car saying that he wanted to show me something. He put me on his lap and let me steer the car.
Ooh, this was fun too! I wanted to call my sisters
Adrian and Genel to the car so that they too could
get a turn. But, he told me I was his favorite girl and
gave me special privileges that my sisters were not
able to enjoy. Little did I know, the grooming had

begun.

I lacked a father figure in my life and I enjoyed his attention. Predators are often quite charming and are quite adept at making their victims feel "special" and adored. This is just what they do. By the time you realize what is happening, you feel as if it is already too late. You begin to feel as though you somehow owe them something. After all, my own father was nowhere in the picture but here this man was willing and ready to step in and provide the love and attention that every little girl wants.

The day came when he managed to get me to the park without my sisters. This time however I was not allowed to get out of the car, and on that day, at the age of five years old, an event took place that put an end to my childhood innocence and would send me in a downward spiral for years to come. It would take years for me to feel clean again.

I never told anyone about what happened to me. We returned to the house and I acted as if everything was normal. The real truth is that from that moment on, I walked through life almost shell-shocked. It was as if I watched myself go through my childhood, going through the motions of first, second, third grade but never really feeling like "one of them." I was angry and jealous of my peers who could give their full attention in school, who were able to sit still, who could concentrate, without their minds wandering off, without the flashbacks, without experiencing nightmares in the daytime, without the fatigue. I was envious of those who had the ability to be "present" and "in the moment."

For me, there was, and is always, this feeling of restlessness, this feeling of being unsettled, almost as if my memories were somehow chasing me and would catch me if I sat still for too long.

I wanted to be free to enjoy the things a young child enjoyed but from the point of my sexual abuse, I have always felt different. It is a feeling of being "unclean," "impure," "tainted," or "soiled." And, if you didn't know it, that absolutely wreaks havoc on a child's self-esteem.

Ms. D and her husband continued to come around and most of the time, I managed to avoid being alone with him. Other days, however, I was not so fortunate. The day came when my sisters and I were invited to spend part of the summer with them in Chicago. I was sick at the thought of being in their home and at his disposal. But what could I do? They had watched me go to the park with him time and time again. They witnessed the joy on my face as I ran to catch up with the chiming ice cream truck after he had given me a few coins. He had convinced me that it was "our" secret as if I was somehow responsible, somehow to blame. I was just a kid and I believed that the chances of anyone believing me if I told were slim to none. I was trapped.

I watched as my mother packed up our things—the lump in my throat growing by the moment. By now I had become a pretty good actress. Inside I was crying but I managed to maintain a front for everyone else. I knew what awaited me when we reached our destination.

I got into the car and waved silently at my moth-er. I knew full well that when I returned, I would be a different person. I wanted to scream out. I wanted to object but the words would not come. On the way to Chicago, they talked on and on about the great time we were going to have and my heart plummeted as we drove closer and closer to our destination. To sweeten the deal, they decided to stop by a clothing store and we were taken on a shopping spree. I was torn between being excited about the new clothes and thinking of the premium that would inevitably have to be paid.

When you are abused by someone you love and trust, you are often filled with feelings of ambiva-lence. You love the person but hate what they are do-ing to you. You know what they are doing is wrong, yet you are seduced by the kind words, the gifts, the special favors that often accompany the abuse.

I lacked the ability to comprehend what was hap-pening to me so I learned to use the situation to my advantage. I tried to regain some semblance of control and became determined to get something for my trouble. Since I was already being used, I learned at a young age to be coy and use my sexuality to my advantage and felt I had sold out. This ultimately served to exacerbate my feelings of worthlessness and self-disgust.

When you suffer sexual abuse, every adult member of the opposite sex becomes suspect. You don't know how or when but you know, sooner or later, they will eventually "go there." Once you have been violated, you come to simply expect it.

It doesn't matter who they are or what office they hold. It could be the janitor, a teacher, a principal, or even a preacher. As parents, we must remain diligent and to protect our children at all costs.

As anticipated, it was a long, difficult summer. I did my best to survive it. Needless to say, I was elated when it was finally over and we were returned to the temple of our familiar. I survived physically but inside my loneliness and feelings of isolation continued to grow. Did you know that you could be lonely even when surrounded by a room full of people? Shame has a way of doing that to you.

Another incident of abuse occurred when I was nine years old. I was "hired" to work at my church every Saturday. Sounds great, doesn't it? What could go wrong in the household of faith? Well, let me tell you, "being in a church doesn't make you a Christian any more that being in a garage makes you a car!" I am not saying this to shine a bad light on the church. I only want to make it clear that predators are everywhere and we must never become complacent or assume anyone is safe or clear. Remember, even Lucifer started off as one of God's angels.

My job was to help clean the church in preparation for Sunday morning worship. Mr. Jim, an esteemed member of the church, was the church's janitor and he volunteered to pay me a couple of dollars each week. I was happy to have the job. It gave me a chance to have my own money—just a couple of dollars a week, but to me it was a big deal.

I marched up the hill each Saturday morning to

report for duty. Everything went well for the first few weeks. I completed the cleaning tasks, received praise and thanks from Mr. Jim, got my money and off I went back down the hill to spend it. It was a good situation until Mr. Jim sought to expand my job duties. It started innocently enough, an occasional rub followed by a rehearsed "oh excuse me." Eventually his advances became more direct. I am ashamed to admit that by then I had grown so accustomed to having the money that I agreed to endure his weekly groping provided it went no further than that. For the second time in my life, I felt I had sold out.

In the early 80's, I recall being impacted by several national news stories. One of those stories was the kidnapping of Adam Walsh who was abducted outside of a mall in Florida. He was reportedly lured to his abductor's car with promises of toys and candy and was found decapitated two weeks later. I can also vividly recall the grip of fear that seized the nation during the period of the Atlanta Child Murders. Within that two- year period, a minimum of twenty-eight African American children, adolescents, and adults were killed. Subsequently, we were warned of the dangers of child abduction. We were taught to never talk to strangers. We knew not to get into a car with people we did not know. We learned to go places in groups as opposed to going alone. We were duly cautioned about stranger danger but were told nothing about handling abuse at the hand of someone that you knew.

We must teach our kids to beware of wolves in sheep's clothing. I was seduced and manipulated by my abusers and because I was a child, I felt that the onus was on me. I felt that because I liked and enjoyed the gifts and attention, that the abuse was my fault. This perpetuated my level of shame and propped the door open for the cycle of abuse to occur again and again in my life. I now know that I lacked the knowledge, the discernment and the self-esteem to protect myself. The fault lies solely with the perpetrator. We must share this message with every child so they will know they are not at fault.

5

Song Sung Blue, Everybody Knows One

As a child, I suffered from intense feelings of isolation and loneliness. Abuse causes you, or at least it caused me, to emotionally retreat from the world. As previously stated, I felt the abuse was my fault. I was ashamed and the very last thing I wanted to do was to reveal that shame to anyone else. Nobody knew of the dark secret I was hiding.

Like Maya Angelou, I know why the caged bird sings. Music was and has been my refuge. As a child, I would turn on the radio and lose myself in the music.

I spent hour upon hour pouring over songs, for in them I found respite from the persistent burden that plagued my soul. I felt less alone as I connected with various artists whose undisguised lyrics spoke directly to what I was experiencing inside. I didn't talk to anyone about my feelings of consuming despondency. Those things weren't talked about back then. But I found a way to express myself through songs such as "Rainy Days and Mondays" by The Carpenters, Judy Garland's "Somewhere Over the Rainbow" reflected my perpetual search for happiness. Smokey Robinson's "The Tracks of My Tears" was really powerful. Think of those lyrics. "Take a good look at my face. You'll see my smile looks out of place. If you look closer, it's easy to trace the tracks of my tears."

When I needed an escape, and Charroy wasn't around to share her music, I turned on the radio. And what or who did I hear? Barry Manilow, Barbra Streisand, Anne Murray, Jim Croce, Helen Reddy, Neil Diamond, Air Supply. I could go on and on but I think you get the picture. I have since branched out and developed an appreciation for other genres but cannot deny my natural affinity for easy listening music. Hey, I lived in Quincy, IL. I'm a product of my environment. Don't judge me.

6

Come and Listen to a Story About a Man Named Ted

My mother met, dated and eventually married a man named Ted. Ted was a member of the Caucasian persuasion. He was a very talented visual artist. He was also a pretty good con artist, but we'll get into that a little bit later. He created some of the most remarkable pieces of art I had ever seen. He wined and dined my mother and her children. He bought us things, gave us money, and took us places we had never been before.

Ted had money, so we had money. We now had a

chance to do some of the things that we couldn't do before. We ventured from the land of barely getting by to the land of more than enough, and boy did we splurge. Ted would give us money to go to the movie theater downtown and get candy and popcorn. Before Ted, the only movie theater candy I would get would be if someone accidentally dropped some on the floor (five second rule). Mom worked hard but we sure weren't spending $2 on a 25 cents box of candy. We just didn't have money to spend like that. But now with Ted, we were in spending heaven. I cannot tell a lie, it was nice.

One day, mom and Ted informed us that we were moving to Chicago, to a deluxe apartment in the sky! Ted promised us a better life. We announced to our friends in the 'hood that we were leaving Quincy and moving to Chicago. We were the envy of all our friends. We packed up and set off for a whole new world. Although my grandmother never said as much, I could somehow sense she was opposed to our move but I was too young to understand why.

Despite her unspoken objections, we were off.

I could not believe we were going to be a family, a real family. We were moving and we would have a mom and a dad living in the same house. That meant more to me than the money, the food and the nice clothes. I felt indebted to Ted that he cared enough about all of us to make it official.

We moved to downtown Chicago and stayed in the Fort Dearborn Hotel. We were enrolled in a school on the South Side of Chicago and found a church home at Quinn Chapel A.M.E. While it was exciting residing at the hotel, I probably saw more than a ten-year-old should have ever seen. We stayed there for six months before making our home on the North Side of Chicago and life began to take on some sense of normalcy.

We moved into a very nice condominium and if the truth be told, I was convinced that we had arrived. I mean there was not a roach in sight. Everything was brand, spanking new. What more could we ask for? We had a nice car and a two-parent family. My new daddy was white. I kind of felt like Louis and Arnold on "Different Strokes" and I touted my white daddy like a badge of pride. We went to the grocery store on a weekly basis and got to pick out whatever we wanted to eat. I got all my favorite cereals and even got to buy pink Nestle Quik—my favorite! The sky was the limit. Ted paid for it all without batting an eye.

I had new clothes. My shirt matched my shoes. I had purses and watches. I made friends and they all thought we were rich because we lived in the "good" neighborhood, and after living in poverty in Quincy, I gladly accepted the role. I further perpetrated the fraud by showing off my white daddy, knowing none of my friends had one of them.

We were treated to exquisite dinners, live theater and my sisters and I were even enrolled in a modeling school in downtown Chicago. Opportunities beyond our wildest dreams were at our fingertips. Our eyes were as big as saucers as we began to think of all we could accomplish, all we could be, all we could achieve here in the great city of Chicago.

7

The Day the Music Died

But the day came when Ted's true colors began to show. Under the guise of parental guidance, he said he needed to prepare me for what was to come later in life. He felt it was his fatherly duty to provide sexual education and believed the hands-on approach was the best method.

I must have been eleven or twelve at the time. You cannot imagine the shame I felt. I was so happy to have a father figure, a daddy, someone who cared about me, someone who wanted to give me the world. I was saddened to discover that he wanted to relegate me to a different role. I was beyond disappointed. I loved this man and was grateful for his presence in my life—so why this? Why couldn't he see that I was just a young girl who wanted and needed a dad? I didn't need confusion, hurt, and pain in my life. Remember, this occurred during a very crucial time in my life. This was during my formative years; a time when my self-identity was being formed. My experience with men thus far had been far from ideal.

In dealing with my step father, I discovered the ambiguity of relationships in that it is quite possible to love and hate a person at the same time. I loved him as a person but absolutely hated what he was doing to me.

This time however, I was determined not to take things lying down (no pun intended). I cried. I begged. I pleaded with him to leave me alone because one: I knew it was wrong, and two: I just wanted a dad. I wanted a father figure to love me for me.

There were nights he would come into my room and I would lay as quiet as possible, barely breathing but inwardly praying he would have a change of heart and just go away. So many nights I prayed, "God please! Where are you? Please hear me. Please help me."

Then there were the times that I would confront him directly, absolutely refusing to comply only to be awakened an hour later and an hour after that until I finally gave in. I wanted peace. I wanted sleep.

I cried. Didn't work. I threatened to tell. Didn't work. I begged for our relationship to go back to the way it was before. Didn't work. I just wanted a dad. But unfortunately, he was too sick, too selfish or too far gone to give me what I needed and wanted most. I even threatened to commit suicide, and when my threats failed to disrupt his recurrent visits, I took an overdose of pills as an attempt to end my life. I became violently ill but obviously, it was a failed attempt. I failed to successfully end my life. I failed to successfully end the sexual abuse. My nightmare continued.

And I never told. I was so bound. I was so

ashamed. Would my mother blame me? Would she hate me? Did I cause this? Did I ask for it? Did I say or wear the wrong thing? Would I ruin things for my family if I told?

In the end, I exercised my right to remain silent and became quite adept at living as though everything in my life was going just fine. I learned to laugh, to put on a smile, to be the life of the party, anything... anything to keep others from finding out my secret shame. If my friends wanted to go hang out, I would hang out. If they wanted to bully other kids, I became a bully. If they wanted to drink, I would drink. At 12-13 years of age, we would put our money together to buy beer and sit around drinking like we were veterans. Our talking and laughing would soon turn into crying as we talked about how bad our lives were. As kids, we were like a bunch of drunks. Many of my friends turned to drugs. Life was too heavy to travel through clean and sober. And if the truth be told, if not for the grace of God, I could have been a drug addict today struggling to get my life together but God had greater things in store for me. He protected me from me. If I would have used something that successfully numbed the pain I was living with, who knows where I would be today. God had His hands on me in the midst of it all.

Soon after starting to drink, I started running with a gang. This gang shall remain nameless lest any of my loyal readers happen to belong to the opposing side. That was a long time ago and I am ready and willing to let bygones be bygones.... but I digress.

We skipped school. We robbed stores. Okay, let me clarify. We did not go in with guns and rob stores. We went into stores under the guise of shopping. I had a long coat with holes in both pockets. I would place the loot in my pockets and it would fall to the bottom of the lining of my coat. We would make trip after trip to various stores. We would go into stores, open packages of food and eat them as we were shopping and leave without paying for them. We would go into clothing stores snatching outfit after outfit, swimsuits and such, whatever our hearts desired without regard for anyone or anything. It was only the grace of God that I never got caught. The scary part is that I didn't really care. Looking back at it now, I can surmise that my life felt so empty, I felt so worthless as a person, no self-esteem, nothing to look forward to, no hopes, dreams, or aspirations so really, what did I have to lose?

I already felt hopeless, useless to society, a screw up so participating in maladaptive behaviors was a reflection of the shame I felt on the inside. It wasn't a stretch for me. I felt horrible on the inside, I acted horrible on the outside.

I made disastrous choices and life exacted a tremendous price. It is true that the wages of sin is death. While I didn't die a natural death, what remained of my innocence was gone with the wind. I no longer had the refuge of my grandmother's home, a home that provided solace from thirsty hands that groped for me. I lost that safe- haven that provided protection from the cold, the hallow stares, the bitter fists that would later batter the various regions of my body. I developed a harshness, a coldness, a dog-eat-dog mentality, a "I'll get you before you get me" mindset. It became a survival of the fittest. And, instead of things getting better, they only grew worse.

8

Life with Mister

We met at a house party. I wasn't his first choice but hey, no worries—the feeling was mutual. But as the night progressed and our paths continued to cross, what should have been a casual conversation morphed into a four-year tumultuous relationship. I gave my all to this relationship. I need to share that I was 12 and Mister was 17. Yes, Mister was much older than I was. Mister had a lot more experience than I did. He was street. He was hood. He became my protector. In all honesty, when all else failed, the begging, the crying, the pleading, the talk of suicide, those things did NOT make the sexual abuse stop. Mister did! Ted, my step father, was terribly afraid of Mister!

I never told Mister about the sexual abuse because he would have, without a doubt, killed Ted. I could not risk that because remember I loved my step-father. I just hated what he did to me. Furthermore, if I told Mister and he went after Ted, my mom and my sisters would find out. I could never risk that. Again, abusers are very good at making you feel somehow responsible and the amount of shame that I carried was tremendous. So, I just let Ted think that Mister knew. On the occasion that Ted would come around, I would drop Mister's name and more times than not, it would do the trick.

The only problem was that Mister was not good to me. I paid a high price for his protection. It started off good. Everybody knew that we were together. A lot of girls liked him because he was older and had a reputation of being a tough guy. Chicago was a rough world and you had to know how to take care of yourself. I wasn't sure if the "windmill" fighting approach would work here in Chicago or not.

Well, Mister would walk me to and from school and was my protection against male and female aggressors. I liked that. I could talk all the smack I wanted to because I knew nobody in middle school would want to step to me. Why would they? I had a boyfriend who was darn near grown!

I didn't have a problem with Mister throwing around his weight and doing what he had to do to protect me from others. The problem came when the ninja started acting out towards me. It started gradually. I can still recall the first slap. It was three or four months into our relationship. We were having a casual conversation. I disagreed with him about something trivial. It was nothing major. I certainly didn't think it was a slappable offense, but out of the blue, he slapped me. I could not believe it. Of course, I cried and threatened to break up with him. The way he reacted to my threats however absolutely won me over. Remember, I was a young, naive, girl with very low self-esteem. He cried, he begged and pleaded for forgiveness. He pledged his undying, lifelong, love for me. Wow. No one had ever felt that way about me before. I was sold to the highest bidder.

This of course was the first of many acts of abuse I suffered at his hands. Sisters, (and brothers), if they hit you once, they will hit you again. Run. Do not pass Go. Do not collect $200. This man was downright cruel and I was a victim of horrendous abuse for five years of my life. He hit me, spit on me, hit me with objects, called me every lowdown, nasty, degrading name in the book, pulled my hair out, banged my head on the floor. It was horrible and I took it. I was dominated by fear. On a couple of occasions, the police were called but I was too terrified to press charges. I feared that he would kill me when he was released. In fact, he would stand there and dare me to have him arrested. He knew they would not keep him locked up long and that I would have hell to pay when he was released. Remember, this was back in the 1980's and the laws were more lenient then. Fortunately, legislation has since been enacted that offers more protection to victims of domestic violence.

Conversely, Mister could be very charming. He had a way of endearing himself to you. He had a smooth as silk singing voice and he wasn't afraid to use it. Although he didn't have much money, he prided himself on giving his special lady gifts, giving gentle and loving touches, making her feel as though she was the most important person in his world. He made you feel needed and loved. We went to Great America, he took me on shopping trips—albeit to the cheapest clothing discount stores in town. He really wooed me. We had matching jogging suits and sweaters. It was cute. I felt so special. However, it was a very confusing time for me. I did not understand that his actions were all a part of the cycle of abuse.

Although I had not told my mother of the physical abuse, she suspected things were not right. She encouraged me to end the relationship but I refused time and time again. She did not realize I had sold my soul to the devil. In many ways, he was my protector and in exchange, I felt I owed him my allegiance. She consulted the judicial system, informing them he was years older than I was, but because he was under the age of 18, he received little more than a stern lecture from the authorities.

Mom turned to the church for help. She consulted with the Pastor who did his best to pray that spirit of rebellion out of me. He went over and beyond the call of duty to help my little wayward behind out. He would even pick me up for school some mornings just to ensure that I continued my education. To him, he was fulfilling his duties as a Pastor by ministering to the needs of his congregation. To me, I became the First Lady! His First Lady was beautiful, fashionable, intelligent, and a strong Black woman. We wanted to walk like her, talk like her. We wanted to be her! On the mornings that my pastor would escort me to school, I would take extra time to primp in the mirror and then saunter out to the car in my most beautiful outfit and then pretend that my darling was driving me to work instead of dropping me off at school. Sick, isn't it?

Poor Pastor was willing to do all he could to help. We would make the usual small talk before he would allow me to do what most teenagers do—turn on the radio. Well, this was our usual routine and things were going along just fine until the day Madonna's "Like a Virgin" came on and I picked that song of all songs to show off my vocal skills. I thought I was jamming. I was hitting all the notes. I happened to look over to see if he was impressed. Instead, he was looking at me as if I had two horns growing out of the top of my head. He insisted that we change the station, saying something about it not being "appropriate." And that was the end of my car rides with my Pastor. Some people are so touchy.

9

Knock, Knock! Who's There?

Another diversionary tactic mom tried was to send me to live with my dad on the South Side of Chicago. I was out of control at home. Maybe, I would respond better to dad. Mister was on the North Side and since dad lived way out South, perhaps the distance would serve to keep us apart. Mister didn't heed mom's warnings to leave her daughter alone so perhaps he would think twice about coming to my father's home. Makes sense, right? Well in some ways, it was my own fault. I was the one who contacted dad when we moved to Chicago.

I really did not "know" my father. As previously mentioned, I could recall only a few occasions that I spent with my father during my youth. When my family and I relocated to Chicago, my mother let us know that our father had no idea that we were returning to the area and that she intended to keep it that way. In one aspect, I understood her instructions and wanted to comply with her orders. In another however, there was something inside of me that longed to connect to this man, this ghost figure, this person who found it so easy to be absent from our lives. Here was a chance to connect to my daddy; my real, living, breathing daddy who did not in fact die the night Chicago died.

One afternoon, my sisters and I were doing laundry at the laundromat. Mom had dropped us off and would return to pick us up when we were finished. While waiting for our laundry to dry, I spied with my little eye a pay phone and underneath the pay phone, a phone book. Being the inquisitive person that I am, I looked through the phone book and found my dad's phone number. I couldn't believe it. There it was in black and white. Here was my chance. I was enthused at the thought of having my dad in my life, especially considering the disappointing way things had turned out with my stepfather. I called my two sisters over and discussed the situation with them. To call or not to call, that was the question. They flat out refused to make the call and tried to talk me out of it. I could tell they were just as anxious as I at the thought of reconnecting with our dad. So, despite the admonition from mom and my own fear of the possibility of rejection, I placed a call to his home and he answered. My plan was to play it cool but before I knew it, I got excited and told him we were now living in Chicago! I stopped short of giving him our address but promised to stay in touch.

We eventually confessed to mom that we had been in contact with dad. She took the news better than expected. She agreed to let us see him when we wanted to, but she didn't want to be involved… fair enough. We saw him on occasion, mainly when he visited us at church. There were times he would pick us up and take us to the South Side to introduce us to yet another sister or brother. The sibling and babies' mama's introductions were endless. It appears that papa was a rolling stone. If it wasn't a sibling, then he was introducing me to yet another uncle or aunt. When I was with my dad, somehow, I always felt like a showpiece. It wasn't as if he knew "me" or was even interested in knowing me. It always felt like he was kind of show-boating. I never felt like I had ever gotten to know him as a person. Our interactions were always somewhat superficial. This wasn't the fairy tale that I thought it would be. I was looking for validation, acceptance, and love. Not being one to give up, I continued to try to forge a relationship with my dad, talking to him on the phone, visiting him when I could. It was fun to announce to friends or anyone who would listen that I was going out South to see my dad! "What are you doing today, Nikkie?" "Oh, I'm going to see my dad!" "Wanna go to the movies?" "Nope, I'm going out to my dad's house." "Tennis anyone? "No, thanks.

Gotta go see … (wait for it) … my dad!"

As I was saying, I went to stay with my dad for a while to put some time and distance between myself and Mister. I could tell dad wasn't used to having a teenager in the home but we were doing our best to make the best of the situation. I took public transportation to the North Side to attend school during the day but returned to his home after school. It was an hour commute but it was no big deal. Many students traveled North to attend school. That's just the way things were done in the city. We were getting established in our daily routine and it seemed to be going on okay.

I didn't have my own room so I slept on the pull-out couch in the living room. I didn't mind. I knew that my dad was in the next room and would be there to protect me should danger pervade the safety of our home. I was with my father. No harm should come nigh me. Or so I thought.

The night came however when I awoke to find my dad nudging me awake and propositioning me for sex. My dad. Not a family friend. Not my step dad this time. Not the church janitor. My dad! I refused his advances but he didn't give up easily. He finally returned to his room, but needless to say, I didn't sleep the rest of the night. How could this be the outcome of a long-awaited relationship with my father? Is this all I was worth as a human being? This message had been reinforced to me again and again. To receive this message from my own biological father was more than I could emotionally handle. More than anything, I really wished I had left well enough alone. I was filled with regret that I had even placed that call from the laundromat. I wished that I had never reconnected with him because then at least I could have had the fantasy of believing that my father sincerely loved me, longed to have a healthy, meaningful relationship with me and wanted the very best for me. At that point, I'd even be willing to accept that he died the night Chicago died. Anything, anything was better than this unbearable truth.

10

They Called Me the Runaway

left my dad's house the very next day but I didn't feel I had a safe place to go. I didn't want to go back home because Mister was not allowed to come around. When he wasn't around, I would have to fight off the advances of my step-father. So, I was just out there. It was rough. Mister and I were bouncing from place to place securing shelter wherever we could find it. I remember many cold desolate nights, walking the streets veering into various restaurants and apartment buildings seeking refuge from the cold. Other times we would resort to jumping the turnstile on the el and riding the train all night to stay warm.

When the winter temperatures became unbearable, Mister came up with a plan to start sneaking me into his mother's apartment after she had gone to bed at night. This worked for a few nights but we were eventually discovered. His mother was like my mother. She didn't play that mess either. She sat us down and explained that while I was welcome to visit on occasion during the day, and while she was home, overnight stays were strictly prohibited.

No worries. Mister had it all worked out. Right around the corner from his mother's apartment was an old, abandoned utility room which would become my nightly dwelling place. It was in the same apartment complex but it had no utilities so it was cold, dark and miserable. Mister had broken the lock in order to gain entry to the room so there was no way to lock the door at night. Mister escorted me to this location night after night and would then return to the safety of his mother's apartment for a nice, warm, comfortable sleep. Yet I was somehow convinced that this man loved me and had my best interest at heart.

I found out through my sisters that some of the members of my family referred to me as "the runaway." I suppose they thought that was funny. It was true-I did run away-but this hurt me nonetheless. They only saw that I ran. No one knew what I ran "from." They just assumed that I was out there, running the streets and being fast. No one could have imagined what horrors I was facing at the hands of my stepfather and now my father. I simply chose what I considered to be the lesser of two, now three, evils. Excuse my candor, but I would rather have chosen to give up the sex than to have it taken from me. I missed my mom and sisters so much. I hated the pain and anguish my absence must have caused them, but I simply did not know what else to do.

I did not feel I could live without Mister's protection, his influence in my life. If he had nothing else, this man had street credibility and I needed that at the time. I was lost. I was broken. I was hurting. If you've never experienced anything like this, it may be hard for you to comprehend.

Walk a mile in my shoes...

See what I see,

Hear what I hear,

Feel what I feel...

Then maybe you'll understand

Why I do what I do...

Till then don't judge me.

11

God Kept Me

Mister and I eventually migrated back up North and found a room for rent in a roach infested, crime ridden motel. Finally, no more walking the streets, looking for unlocked buildings where we could borrow minutes or even seconds of warmth from the cold. Fast food restaurants had grown unfriendly to the plight of homeless youth and demanded that you make a purchase in order to frequent their establishments. Even if you were fortunate enough to get enough change together for a burger, one could only nibble for so long before they expected you to wrap it up and head on out the side door.

Our weekly rent was due every Friday and let's just say the phrase "robbing Peter to pay Paul" took on new meaning. Mister was nothing if not creative and he had a few ideas on how to survive. We were planning to run a scheme on someone. The plan was to hitch a ride and once we got in the car, Mister was going to rob him. Now let's look at this thing. I'm from Small town, USA. I don't know nothing about that life. I listen to easy listening music; love me some Barry Manilow and Barbra Streisand, so how in the world did I end up in a situation like this? Where does that happen? Again, I digress.

So, our little scheme was going as planned until it was time for us to make our escape. The car had automatic locks and when it was time to get out, Mister got out, but my timing was off (of course because I'm not about that life). Mister takes off running, but I'm trapped in the car. Our chauffeur drove me to a nearby cemetery and proceeded to take out his frustrations on me. The streets don't care whether you are new to the game or not. He was furious and I seriously thought he was going to kill me. I tried all I could to talk my way out of the situation but he wasn't having it. He felt duped and he wanted vengeance. He talked about the different ways he could punish me, whether he should kill me or use me to work the streets and make him some money. I prayed. I mean, I really prayed.

I knew I needed to get out of that car and I knew that I was running out of time. I begged and pleaded that he spare my life, all the while waiting for the right moment to make my escape. Something deep inside told me that I would get one chance and that I could not afford to mess it up. I carefully waited for what I thought was the right moment. Something caught my abductor's attention to the left and when he turned to look, I hit the lock and lunged for the door. He reached for me, but this time, my timing was right. I flew through that graveyard, refusing to turn around to see if he was in pursuit. One: I was motivated by the fear of him catching me, and two: I was motivated by my fear of one of those corpses getting up out of those graves. I don't play with dead people. I was gone!

I exited at the other side of the graveyard and boarded a city bus. I didn't have a dime to my name but boarded the bus anyway. I hurriedly told the bus driver I was just kidnapped and begged him to let me on the bus and to leave the area quickly. Without hesitation, he encouraged me to sit down right behind him and tore away from the curb. I never saw my captor again.

Somehow, I was able to resume my eighth-grade studies in the midst of all that chaos. I guess deep down inside, a part of me knew that that situation, that circumstance, was not where I belonged. "That" would not be my destiny and it was important for me to continue to receive my education. My school assumed I was still living at home and I made no mention otherwise. I managed to graduate from eighth grade. My sister Adrian was the only family member to attend my graduation. No one else knew of my whereabouts. I swore her to secrecy as I was bound and determined not to return home. I was heartbroken to be estranged from my mother but I was equally glad to be free from Ted. Furthermore, Mister had me convinced that my place was with him and that he would protect me from all hurt, harm, and danger.

12

Do You Know Where You're Going To?

got pregnant at the age of 14. I could not feign surprise. I was out there doing what grown folk did, without taking proper precautions. It was plain and simple. Tongues wagged and I could tell that many expected me to be embarrassed and ashamed. Perhaps that should have been my response, but because of the years of self-loathing I had already endured, teen pregnancy measured pretty low on the Richter Scale of humiliation. To be honest, a part of me longed to have something, someone to call my own.

I had no idea what I was doing. I only knew that I was on a fast course to nowhere and that this little being that I was now responsible for needed me in a way that I had never been needed before. He gave me a reason to do better, be better, want better.

Because of my age, I was considered to be a high-risk pregnancy. I also knew that if I continued living in that stressful environment, the chances of giving birth to a healthy baby were further decreased. I reached out to my mother, and like the prodigal son, I was welcomed me back home again. I knew she didn't grow happy feelings for my son's father overnight. Her disdain for him remained. What I saw in her however was a willingness to choose love instead of anger for the sake of her daughter and unborn grandchild. She loved us so much that she was willing to take the good with the bad. She loved me enough that she put aside her feelings to ensure our safety. That's a mother's love. I saw her as she clung to God, reaching out to Him desperately for guidance and direction, sought out the advice and prayers of her mother, just for me. That's a mother's love. Her prayers did not go unnoticed.

I became more focused in school as I knew that it was no longer just about me. I knew that the decisions I made from then on affected both myself and my baby. My scholastic efforts did not go unnoticed. My grades greatly improved and I received an award for my academic achievements. I remember looking out into the audience and locking eyes with my English teacher, the one who recommended me for the award. In spite of my situation, she saw something in me at the time that I had not seen in myself. She believed in me. In her eyes, I saw pride. She saw not where and who I was at that time, but who I would one day become.

I went to every prenatal appointment and followed the doctor's orders to the best of my ability. I was determined to give birth to a healthy baby.

On July 13, 1985, I went into labor. I did not have a job so the only insurance I had was issued through the state of Illinois Public Aid program. Back then, you didn't get to choose which hospital you wanted to give birth in. If you were uninsured and living in Chicago, you were going to Cook County Hospital. That meant you did not have the luxury of laboring at the hospital. You labored at home. I had been warned not to arrive at the hospital too early or else I would run the risk of being sent back home. I knew that I would not have the comfort of having a nice nurse who coaxed me kindly through the process, gently wiping my brow and bringing me ice chips to satisfy my parched throat.

To say that I was not prepared is an understatement. For those of you who are old enough, think Sigourney Weaver in the movie *Alien*. I had no idea who or what was taking over my body. And the pain, oh the pain! All I could do was roll back and forth on the floor in deep travail. How long, Lord? How long?

Finally, it was time to make our way to the hospital. The ride was long and difficult and I spent the entire time praying that they would put me out of my misery upon arrival. And please Lord, do not let them send me back home.

They agreed to admit me but instead of sending me to a room, I was sent to a ward where there were several other women in labor. The only thing that separated each bed was a curtain. I was mortified but by then contractions started speaking in an unknown language. I was in so much pain that my modesty went right out the window. At one point, I told one of those sisters to quiet down. It was my time to scream. My dignity was gone. I got in position. I didn't care if the entire hospital—including the janitorial staff—assisted with the delivery. I just wanted this baby out of me.

After laboring for fourteen hours, I gave birth to a healthy baby boy who I named Richard. I was a child who had just given birth to a child. I had no idea what I was doing. I only knew that I loved this little fellow and that I needed to do all that I could to provide a decent life for him.

I continued in school and worked to take care of myself and my baby. I eventually left my mother's home and moved in with Richard's father. My school and work attendance became sporadic at best as he often chose what days he would or would not provide child care to our son. His cooperation was based upon his many mood swings or if he felt the need to punish me for some random reason. No babysitter, no school. I eventually had to drop out.

Mister was mentally and physically abusive. He quite honestly was the cruelest person I had ever met. The slightest thing would cause him to escalate. His moods were unpredictable. He was like the weather. The sun could be out, not a cloud in the sky. You would assume it was going to be a lovely day, but suddenly you detect a slight shift in the wind and before you knew it, a torrential thunderstorm would appear out of nowhere.

He and I could be together and having a good day and then suddenly I would sense a tiny change in his mood. I knew if I could not turn it around, whatever the "it" was, it was going to be a bad night. I would go into overdrive to change the subject, change the radio station, change the channel, change my outfit, change the weather (if I could)—anything to avoid a beating. I would speak softly, speak louder, cook food, buy food, sing to him, hell, I would even try to rap, offer sex, anything to avoid a fight. But once he was in "the zone," he could not be talked down. It was as if he had this insurmountable energy or rage that had to be expended or else. I felt like I was with David Banner AKA 'The Incredible Hulk' and that once he started to turn green, it was all she wrote.

He would beat me mercilessly and then brag to his friends that I could barely move due to one of his punishments. The man had no shame. No worries. I had plenty for the both of us.

There were times that I would boil water to make Richard's baby formula and yes, I thought to pour it all over his daddy. But again, I knew that he held my life in his hands. He had the power to take my life. I saw him as all-powerful. I was terrified of this man. I had witnessed the blackness, the emptiness, the cold-ness in his eyes as he offered blow after blow until his wrath was spent.

My abuser was strategic in his beatings. He did not batter me in places that could be detected. I never once suffered a black eye or a busted lip. The damage was always sustained in places throughout my body that was covered by clothing. I took great strides to hide the welts and bruises that covered my body after surviving his beatings. Performing simple tasks such as bending over to change my son's diaper would cause severe muscle spasms for days following one of his attacks. I was repeatedly assaulted throughout my body as if he were fighting a grown man. He would hit me with mops, brooms, dustpans, anything that was within his reach. It didn't even have to make sense. He would pick it up and beat me with it. On one occasion, he used our son's walker as a weapon against me, beating me until it fell apart.

Over time, his fits of rage grew progressively worse. There were times that I threatened to leave. One such occasion, during the winter, my mom purchased a brand-new coat for me. Mister and I had gotten into an argument, which resulted in him slapping me. Throughout the course of the argument, I said I was tired of the situation and wanted it to end. I left to go to school the next day and when I returned, I discovered he had taken a knife and slashed all my clothing—including the brand-new coat that I hadn't even had the chance to wear. He promised to do the same to me should I ever talk about leaving again. That was a new low even for him. I was scared for my life. I was also so ashamed to admit to my mother that I was in this abusive relationship and that he had torn up the coat she purchased for me. I felt like such a failure. How could I be in this situation? I was a teenage parent living with a man who beat me. I felt like such a pitiful loser. So, I kept it all to myself and the cycle of violence continued.

Although the physical violence did not extend to our son, the atmosphere of the home was fraught with tension. Richard began to react to the acts of violence as well as the stress and tension that infiltrated our home. I recall those occasions when he would stand in his crib, wide eyed and screaming. I would beg his father to stop assaulting me, if only for the sake of our son. He seemed unable or unwilling to control his rage. This served as the catalyst for my departure. Although I did not consider myself worthy of a better life, I knew that this innocent baby deserved more than to be raised in this abusive household. Richard birthed in me a desire to break free from the chains that held me captive for far too long.

I knew I had to get out carefully and quickly. One afternoon while Mister was at work, I hastily shoved as many things as I could into a few garbage bags and left. Having no money, I went to the only place that I could—my mother's house. It was then that I had to share with her the full scope of the abuse I had endured. Though Ted was still present in the home, I had returned hardened, angry and a less likely target for his sexual advances.

13

Not Without a Fight

I t did not take him long to discover where I had gone... and the stalking began. Mister called my mother's home several times a day. He made sure that I was fully aware that he was constantly watching our home and that I was not safe. He knew who was coming and going at all times of the day. He made threats to kill me and everybody in the home unless Richard and I came back to him. I called the police on several occasions but they refused to get involved until a "real crime" had been committed. Until he actually followed through on the threats, they would not intervene.

I lived in constant fear for my family's safety. I was terribly humiliated to bring this threat of harm to my mother's home and considered returning to him just to make him back off. This is a common reason that women return to their abusers. By now, however, my mother was determined to help me get away from him.

A couple of weeks had gone by and my sister Adrian and good friend Kacia invited me to go to the mall. I had not stepped one foot out of the house for fear that this man would catch me. After several objections, I finally agreed to go with them. They reasoned that surely, he could not be watching my house after "all this time."

I decided to go, and after leaving the house and walking about a block, I looked up to discover Mister walking straight towards me. My body instantly grew cold. I quickly looked to the left and the right, not knowing where to go or what to do. My sister looked at me and yelled, "Run!" and I ran. I ran as fast as my legs would carry me. I was running for my life. I ran towards a neighbor's apartment.

She lived on the second floor and I ran through the alley, up two flights of wooden stairs. Before I reached the landing, however, he caught hold of my foot and drug me back down the stairs severely scraping the skin off my back as I made my descent. Adrian and Kacia did their best to fight him off but they were no match against this madman who felt that I belonged to him.

My life teetered in his hands as I witnessed the all too familiar rage and anger in his eyes. I waited to see what punishment he would mete out for all the unanswered calls and refusals to return home. I was not ready to die so I began to pray and beg him to let me go. Adrian and Kacia were beside themselves with fear. I vacillated between wanting them to somehow help me and wanting them to run for their own lives.

I knew full well that he could and would do serious harm to all of us. Strangely enough, on what could have been my last day on earth, something totally unexpected happened. He grabbed me, held onto me and began to sob, begging my forgiveness and asking me to come back home. This may not mean much to you all, but this was a miracle to me. This certainly was not his style. He kicked butt and asked questions later. I knew that the police had already been called so all I had to do was stall. I began to lay it on as thick as he was. He loved me? Well, I loved him too! He wanted me to come back home? Well, all he had to do was ask! I got real scriptural with a brother, "Come let us reason together."

I talked a good game but I knew better than to leave with him. I knew deep down inside he was boiling with frustration and that this was all a ruse to get me to return home. By the time I was done running my mouth, the police had mercifully arrived and Mister had run off without me. God had given me wisdom that day. I had to stop crying, stop panicking, and to start listening. I needed an answer, a remedy to my problem, and as the old saints say, "He may not come when you want Him but He's right on time." God gave me victory in that situation and you know what, I survived!

Not one to give up, my abuser continued to harass and stalk me. I lived in tremendous fear not only for myself but for my family as well. I could not go on living this way. I couldn't eat. I couldn't sleep. I was afraid to go outside. I was afraid every time one of my family members left the house. I felt I was putting all of us at risk by continuing to stay there. I knew that something needed to change.

14

A Change is Gonna Come

have a childhood friend named Resha. She and I had kept in contact through letters and the occasional phone call (long distance was not free back then). When she learned what my son and I were going through, something inside of her rose up. I didn't know it then. I now know that it was the spirit of God.

She began speaking words of life to me. She spoke words of love and comfort. She was caring and compassionate. She reminded me of my worth and somehow those words penetrated the shroud of darkness, the cloak of shame that I had worn for many years. At the end of the call, she let me know that I could always come back home to Quincy, IL, and start over again.

So, at the age of sixteen years old, with a baby on my hip, a garbage bag of clothing in my hand, I boarded the Amtrak train and headed out of my situation and went back home. Resha made me believe that even at my lowest point, I could get back up again.

I wish I could say that I went back to Quincy and lived happily ever after. We all know that life never happens that way. I had been with my son's father long enough for him to know my connection to Quincy. I didn't get a chance to breathe a sigh of relief because before I had a chance to settle in, I was accosted by him one afternoon. I was out running errands as he came up behind me, stuck the point of a pocket-knife in my back and said these words that have echoed in my mind for many years, "bitch walk!" I did exactly as I was told. I was panicked and frightened as I was ushered passed places all very familiar to me. This was my hometown, my old stomping grounds. I mistakenly assumed I was safe here. Yet, he marched me right passed my aunt's house and my uncle's car detailing business. I considered trying to make a run for it or at the very least drawing attention to the myself. He must have known what I was thinking because he warned me if I tried to go anywhere or do anything, he would slash my throat on the spot. He reminded me that he had nothing to lose. So, I conceded.

We reached a location where he had secured a room, and from the looks of it, he was prepared to stay there as long as necessary. He proceeded to beat and rape me as punishment for the months of ignoring him. This time my fake promises of returning to him and resuming the relationship profited me nothing. He was on to my empty vows of reconciliation. The jig was up. But something inside of me refused to give up. I refused to quit. I continued to work, to try to convince him that it was he and I against the world, that we belonged together and that this time, nothing and no one would tear us apart.

Eventually, I wore away at his resistance and mistrust. I agreed to return to Chicago with him but reasoned that there was no way we could be together while leaving our son behind. Furthermore, I argued that if I failed to pick up our son from daycare, the police would inevitably be notified. He agreed to allow me to pick up our son and to stop by grandmother's home to retrieve needed clothes and supplies. He warned he would be right outside and would kill all of us should I try anything. I assured him that I could be trusted and that I wanted to be with him just as much as he wanted to be with me. I even gave him a kiss for good measure.

I walked into my grandmother's home. She was furious as I was several hours late. I quickly made her aware of the situation at hand. I begged her not to get involved because I was terrified he would hurt her as well. I told her he was outside waiting and expected me to be back out in five minutes. I asked her to conspicuously call the police as I made a show of packing our belongings. I reiterated the fact that she was not to get directly involved. I knew just how dangerous Mister could be.

Nobody told me "grandma" means "Madea" in Ebonics! In her kitchen, right behind her garbage can stood a long-handled axe. My longsuffering, card-carrying, Bible quoting grandma grabbed said axe and ran out the front door toward Mister yelling all manner of expletives at him. And would you believe it? He ran off. I just stood there absolutely astounded. I could not believe what I had just witnessed. Picture "Granny" from the Beverly Hillbillies and you'll get a good visual of the physique of my little grandma. But right then and there, she faced that Goliath and won.

I didn't realize it at the time but my grandma had something I didn't know she had. She had an unshakable faith in God. She knew that God had given her victory before and if He had done it before, He could certainly do it again. She had faith because of the battles He had already won. She knew she didn't have to fear because the Lord her God was strong and mighty. I saw a small, frail woman but Mister must have seen a host of angels encamped around her and he knew that he was outnumbered, and he fled.

Mister never returned and as the weeks and months went by, the constant fear and threat of harm began to subside as my sense of security began to grow. Mister phoned sporadically throughout the years which was always a concern for me. I was never quite sure how he managed to learn of my where-abouts and I never knew if his phone calls would lead to his return in our lives. Fortunately his harassment did not extend beyond the telephone and in time, I was able to live in peace.

15

More About Resha...

Resha and I have been friends since pre-school. She is one of the kids I used to pick on all the time. However, the day that Resha learned to fight back and win was the day she became my best friend. I couldn't have her going around saying that she whooped me so wisdom demanded that I put her on my team. We've been cool since then.

Resha and I maintained our relationship even after my family moved to Chicago. We've always kept in touch. Resha developed mad singing skills when

I was away. Low key, I thought we could both sing, but when I came back home, she was singing all over Quincy, leading solos in church, singing at weddings, funerals, etc. I sat in the audience time after time, smiling and clapping, but I was really kind of thinking, "Wait a minute, how did this happen? We used to be on the same level?" Anyway! Well, while I was gone, a change took place in Resha's life. The tone of our conversations started to change and she began to talk to me about her relationship with Jesus, how he made a difference in her life, and how he could make a difference in mine as well. Listen, it's one thing for a person to tell you about Jesus, it's another thing for them to show you Jesus. If I was a trip and Resha was on my team, one could conclude that Resha was a trip too. Birds of a feather generally flock together. But this girl had changed so much from the girl I once knew that I was convinced that Jesus was real. Her transformation sealed the deal. Through her lifestyle, she showed me Jesus.

Once I was home, Resha went into overdrive. I

was sincere in making some changes when I moved back to Quincy but I wasn't planning to do so right away. But Resha was relentless and invited me to church every single week. Church, church, church! Jesus, Jesus, Jesus was all Resha talked about. And those below the knee, blue jean skirts really had to go. If she thought I was giving up my mini-skirts, she had another thing coming.

We used to pass notes in the hallway in high school and she wrote me letter after letter trying to convince me of God's love for me. I didn't open half of them because my flesh was looking for juicy gossip and you weren't getting that with Resha. They were all full of scripture.

I finally went to church with Resha just to get her off my back, and an amazing thing happened. I found what was missing in my life. I found this Jesus that Resha was talking about and my life began to change. I discovered that true contentment could only be achieved through a relationship with God. Having a relationship with God became so important to me. I was hungry to know more and more about Him and His will for my life. I began to see a bigger plan and purpose for my life.

One of the first scriptures I learned was Jeremiah 29:11, "'For I know the plans that I have for you,' declares the Lord, 'plans to prosper you and not harm you, plans to give you hope and a future.'" These words began to take root in my heart. I began to believe them. Perhaps my life was not ruined. Perhaps God could still use me. Despite what I had endured, despite what I had done, perhaps there was some good that remained in me. God had a purpose for me, plans to prosper and not harm me. Those words gave me life.

I had a new story. I had a new song. I had gone through my own personal hell but yet, I survived! Although my relationship with my biological father was lacking, my heavenly Father not only loved me but He was in my corner. He wanted the best for me. He was rooting for me, cheering me on, assuring me of His love for me—all the things I wanted from my earthly father.

I was grateful for this new found freedom I found in Christ and thankful for Resha for being so darn persistent! Resha continues to be one of my closest friends and I look to her for strength, prayer, support and guidance.

16

Open Arms

joined the church where Resha attended which was then called Pilgrim Baptist Church and jumped in with both feet. I went to church on Sunday morning and Sunday night. I even went back for Wednesday night Bible study. My favorite part of the church service was Praise and Worship where I was able to connect to God in a very real way. It was as though my songs of worship went directly from my lips to God's ears. I felt rejuvenated, clean and whole as I was amazed to discover that God loved me and desired to be in relationship with me. I had never experienced anything like this and needless to say, I was "all in".

I lived with my grandma at the time and while I knew she was happy with the changes that were taking place in my life, I also sensed an unspoken level of uneasiness. At the time, I thought she was angry because I left the A.M.E. Church which had been our family denomination for many years. I later discovered she was afraid I was being brainwashed and manipulated. In hindsight, I cannot fault her for her concern because the changes in me were extreme. I was zealous in my pursuit for God and I routinely participated in church shut-in's and fasting rituals.

Dissension arose due to our continued theological differences and it all came to a head one day as grandma chided me on my unhealthy weight loss which was caused by too much fasting. I felt I had heard enough and decided I was going to move out of grandma's house. She simply did not understand my spiritual journey! Operation shop for a new place to live was in full effect. Problem was, I didn't have any money. It was during that time that I met Sheila Vaughn who was also a member of Pilgrim Baptist. Sheila was a fire cracker of a woman and our spirits connected instantly. She was older than I was so I looked up to her as an older sister/mother figure. She had a son named Jamar. She and Jamar welcomed both Richard and I into their home with open arms-after she sat down and met with my grandma to make sure grandma was okay with the move. Sheila believes in doing things in decency and in order.

It was a wonderful blending of both families and I was thrilled to live with someone who shared my religious beliefs. Things were going along swimmingly until...I realized Sheila had boundaries, questions and rules too. What the what? She wanted to know where I was going, with whom and what time I would be coming back? I got that type of treatment at grandma's house. What I failed to realize was that although I had given my life to Christ, I was still human. I was the common denominator in this equation and I had a lot of growing up to do.

You can move from one place to another but when you get there, there you'll be. You cannot out-run yourself for you will discover that you take your problems, your issues with you wherever you go. There is no such thing as a geographical cure so it's best to deal with "you" wherever "you" are instead of trying to elude the situation.

Sheila's role in my life was very instrumental. She held on to me when I was kicking and screaming, try-ing to make my way through young adulthood and through life as a single mother. I appreciate her for her willingness to take me in and give me a chance when I am sure others around her discouraged her from doing so. She saw something in me that she considered "good ground" and worthy of her time, energy and investment. The Bible says, "By this men will know that you're my disciples that you have love one for another." Thank you, Sheila Vaughn (Bell) for putting your love into action for me and for my Richard. I wouldn't be who I am today without you. I love you! By the way, I know it was you who sent

me the unmarked envelopes of money while I was a
student at W.I.U. You're simply the best!!!

her own!

Jimmy was very popular in high school. He was a starter on the Quincy High School (QHS) basketball team and he was a star. Everybody loved him. He lit up the crowd every time he was on the court. I watched every move he made and cheered like crazy when he made a basket. His jump shot was out of this world! The cheerleaders did their thing on the sidelines, but no worries, I held it down in the stands! I made my presence known.

Each night after the QHS Blue Devils played a home game, the fans would congregate at a local fast food restaurant and wait for the players to come in. I sat on pins and needles until #4, Mr. Blue Devil himself made his way into the restaurant. Here he came, Jimmy Bailey, wearing a pair of Levi blue jeans, an Adidas jacket, white baseball cap and always the latest gym shoes. Be still my beating heart. (I am cheesing as I walk down memory lane). He would order his food and take a seat. Please God, let him sit somewhere in my section! I mean, I wore my black jeans with the gold paisley pattern, black turtle neck sweater, riding boots and slept in pink foam rollers the night before to make sure my curls held just right. Please Lord, let it pay off. I had even touched up my .99 Wet 'n Wild lipstick before he walked in.

It worked! He sat right next to me and we talked and laughed the entire time. The party would continue to his house afterwards as I, along with several others, would hang out well into the night. He would hold court the entire time. He was hilarious.

That was the beginning of our friendship, which eventually grew into a wonderful love affair. He graduated from Quincy High and went off to school in Chicago. We maintained our relationship through phone calls and letters. We always looked forward to reconnecting during holidays and school breaks. We managed to maintain our connection in spite of the distance.

This was somewhat of a confusing time for me. I loved God and this wonderful new relationship that I had with him but I also loved my Jimmy. Was it okay to be in a relationship? Was I betraying God because I was dating and actually enjoying myself in life? I was still going to church but I was back to eating again as opposed to fasting all the time. Was I still saved? That was a question I was asked often by well-meaning (I think) church folk. Was Jimmy saved? Was he baptized in the Holy Ghost with the evidence of speaking in tongues? I don't know. Let me ask him. I am surprised our relationship survived throughout that time as I wrote him many letters explaining why we could not be together since we were "unequally yoked." It was such a confusing time for me but my Jimmy was persistent and never gave up. I am glad that he didn't.

I continued my high school education at Quincy Senior High. I was in my senior year by then. One afternoon, my English teacher announced he was taking a group of students to Macomb, IL, to visit the campus of Western Illinois University. He extended the invitation to senior students who were interested in attending college. I was a teenage parent and the idea of going to college was far beyond my imagination. I only agreed to go to escape a day of monotonous classes.

I listened to various faculty members discuss the application process as well as touting the benefits of attending W.I.U. I feigned interest as they discussed the different academic offerings, even specifying my field of interest when called upon. I saw and heard everything the university had to offer but I didn't believe any of it was within my reach.

Later that day, my English teacher pulled me away from my friends, looked me in my eyes and told me that I could do this. I thanked him for the trip to W.I.U. and explained to him all the reasons why this opportunity was not possible for me.

I was a teenage parent, I had no money, and my grades were not as good as the other students' grades. I finally confessed that I only went on the trip to get out of classes that day. He said he was aware of that all along but that did not change the fact that I was quite capable of earning my college degree.

His confidence in me, his ability to see something in me that I could not see in myself, coupled with the promise of Jeremiah 29:11, served as the motivation for me to complete high school, take my ACT, apply and get accepted into Western Illinois University. Getting accepted was the easy part. Turning the dream into a reality took some work. As the Bible says, faith without works is dead. I came up with a checklist and addressed each obstacle one step at a time. I had no job at the time and therefore very little money. I depended on the monthly welfare check I received to support myself and my then three-year-old son.

While scanning the local classified ads one afternoon, I discovered a car for sale for $500. I knew I needed a car but $500 might as well have been $5000 because I did not have the money. That same car was listed in the classified section the following week. Obviously, there were no takers for the $500 price. I called to inquire about the car. It had some issues but so did I so I figured we would get along just fine.

I explained my situation to the seller and asked her to consider working with me on the price of the car. In the end, she agreed to sell me the car for $250. I did not have $250 but she allowed me to make payments until the car was paid in full. I fulfilled my obligation and in August of 1988, loaded my worldly possessions into that $250 car and off my son and I went to Macomb, IL., the home of Western Illinois University.

I must admit I was driving into the unknown, but driving nonetheless. Dr. Maya Angelou in *Wouldn't Take Nothing for My Journey Now* says, "Each of us has the right and the responsibility to assess the roads which lie ahead, and those over which we have traveled, and if the future road looms ominous or unpromising, and the roads back uninviting, then we need to gather our resolve and, carrying only the necessary baggage, step off that road into another direction. If the new choice is also unpalatable, without embarrassment, we must be ready to change that as well." With those powerful, life changing words in my mind, I was going for it.

I knew the road that was behind me was certainly uninviting. I wanted and needed something different, and with God's help, I was willing to do what was necessary to make a difference in our lives. Some make the mistake of waiting for God to just drop blessings in our laps. While God can do that, I believe that God helps us to help ourselves. We have a responsibility to take part in our own healing, our own victory, our own restoration. This is why, after seeing the man lying at the pool of Bethesda for 38 long years, Jesus asks him, "will thou be made whole? If so, then rise up, take up thy bed and walk." We play a crucial role in fulfilling our destiny. We must choose to rise up, take up our bed, and walk (John 5).

18

Life at WIU

ut it didn't come easy. I'm not saying that I was not scared. I was. I would like to tell you that we made it to campus and all the pieces magically fell into place. They didn't. We all know that life is never that simple. My son and I moved into Married and Single Parent Housing. As I arrived on campus and unpacked our meager belongings, I took my son by the hand and walked around the campus familiarizing myself with our new environment. I watched the excitement of my fellow students as they moved into the dorms. Most appeared overjoyed at the prospect of living on their own as they looked forward to gaining a sense of freedom from the restraint of their parents. I, on the other hand, was filled with reservations and fear. Could I pull this off? Could I make this work? How would I feed myself and my child? Did I have what it took to earn a degree? Did I really belong? Did I make the right decision?

These doubts and questions can and will come. I made the decision to face the fear and do it anyway. I knew that my son and I had a much better chance of surviving if I earned my college degree so I made the decision to stay and fight for our futures.

At times, we ran out of food so I became acquainted with the local food pantry. Other single mothers and I relied on each other for child care needs when the daycares were closed. At times, I ran out of money for daycare. I volunteered at the daycare until the balance was back at zero. I was determined to do what I had to do, when I had to do it. Giving up was not an option. Throughout my times of struggle, I learned that God will not always move a mountain out of your way, but He will give you strength to climb the mountain. Sometimes you just have to hold on, keep the faith, keep pressing until your change comes.

In the words of Pastor James C. Bailey, when all else fails and you find yourself at the end of your rope, tie a knot and hold on until your change comes. Sooner than later God will step in and fix your situation. All you have to do in the meantime is hold on!

19

My Boaz

ookie here! Lookie here! Here comes Jimmy Bailey swinging through to visit his Nikkie in Macomb, the home of WIU. His visits became more and more frequent. Try as he might, he just could not stay away. We were crazy about each other. But a visit was one thing, living together was a whole 'nother. We knew that shacking wasn't an option because the scriptures said it's better to marry than to burn. Neither one of us cared for the heat too much so we decided to do this the right way. We loved each other so why wait?

I took a break from my morning classes. We stopped by a jewelry store to purchase wedding bands. We went to the McDonough County Courthouse, talked some guy into being our witness, paid the clerk and said our "I do's." He was 21 years old and I was 19. We grabbed a quick sandwich, smooched a little in the car and I was off to attend my afternoon classes. Okay, we celebrated a little that night but it ain't that kind of book so go on somewhere! Go read you some Zane or something.

When this young brother said "I do", he meant it. He took his responsibilities seriously. I figured that marriage was an extension of our boyfriend and girl-friend relationship; kind of like a stamp of approval. No biggie. But he stepped in and stepped up, work-ing two to three jobs at a time making sure that Rich-ard and I had everything we needed. He became a provider, a nurturer, a doctor, a supporter, a father, a disciplinarian, a cook, a tutor, a mechanic, anything that we needed him to be. He became a wonderful parent to our son Richard. He loved him and fathered him with a love unparalleled to any fatherly love I had ever seen. We were immensely blessed to have him in our lives.

20

The Saga Continues

Having Jimmy with us provided the support I needed to better focus on my studies. I had always done well in my courses but was much less stressed with him in our lives. I did have problems with one course in particular. It was Statistics. I needed to pass Statistics to earn my degree. I failed the course once at WIU. But I refused to be denied. I met with my advisor and requested permission to take the same class at the local junior college. I reasoned that if I passed the class, I could have the credits transferred to WIU. My proposal was approved.

I met with the professor before the class began and let him know that I had worked too hard and come too far to not earn my college degree. I warned him that I would have many questions, was willing to do extra credit, and was even prepared to work with a tutor. Failing this class was not an option.

The class sizes were much smaller at the junior college. I was persistent, attended every class and took thorough notes. I followed through on my promise to ask several clarifying questions and met with my professor after each quiz and exam to track my progress. I did not pass the class with flying colors, but I passed. Truth be told, he may have let me out with a passing grade to avoid seeing me again the following semester. I didn't really care. I passed. Like the late Malcolm X says, some things you have to take by "any means necessary." I'll take those three transferrable college credits sir and be on my way back to W.I.U. Have a fantastic summer!!!

I graduated from WIU on time and with honors! I worked really hard to earn my degree and to maintain a good GPA in the process. I refused to allow that Statistics class to derail my dreams and thus prevent me from accomplishing my goals. It wasn't easy but I knew that anything worth having was worth fighting for. Following graduation, my original intent was to attend law school but we returned to Quincy where I accepted an internship at the Probation Department. There I interviewed individuals who were arrested for various levels of crimes ranging from retail theft to first degree murder. I was intrigued by what motivated people to commit crime and if certain environmental factors could change their propensity to engage in criminal activity.

After completing my internship, I accepted a position as a Youth Counselor at a residential home for emotionally and behaviorally challenged teens. I found this position to be very challenging but I welcomed the opportunity to make a difference in the lives of those less fortunate. I have spent most my career in Social Services. I have worked with both youth and adults.

The most rewarding time of my career was when I worked as a Substance Abuse Therapist. I counseled women who were dually diagnosed—that meant they suffered from both a chemical dependency as well as a mental health disorder(s). If you had the privilege of listening to their life histories, the common thread of abuse, of hurt, of disappointment, of rejection, it was easier to understand how one might turn to the use of alcohol and other drugs to cope with the pain of this life. I served these women with all I had in me, fully recognizing that there but for the grace of God, go I. I could have easily been the resident and not the counselor. I knew that pain of which they spoke. If I would have found something that effectively numbed that pain, I don't know if I would have found the strength to put it back down. All I can say is that God kept me. He protected me from me. It wasn't the first time He has done it. Let me explain.

21

North End Disco

On 10th and Elm Street, which we referred to as "Dime Street," there was a tavern called the North End Disco. When I was growing up, all the grown folks hung out at the North End Disco and occasionally, mom would send one of us kids there to relay a message to this or that person. I would be the first one to volunteer to run the errand for her because I could not wait to set foot inside the disco and even when she didn't send one of us, I along with my sisters and friends would find some reason to walk by the disco to sneak a peek at what was going on.

I am telling you, something happened to me every time I stepped foot in the disco. From the smell of stale popcorn, beer and cigarettes, all the way down to the holes in the floor, I loved the North End Disco. And I could not wait until I got old enough to party at the disco. Each Friday and Saturday night, I made my way up towards the disco to see who wore what and who was with who at the North End Disco. I knew that one day I would be old enough to dress up and go to the disco myself.

Man, when my time finally arrived, I had myself a ball! My friends and I took all week deciding what we would wear. The weekend finally came and we kicked it! I mean we would dance until we sweated out our new hairdos, wrinkled our new layaway outfits and the icing on the cake—I mean the measure of a good evening—was in seeing who was gonna fight who that night. We couldn't just go out and have a good time. It was a really good night when the night ended with a fight. We needed something to eclipse our night; something that we could talk about the rest of the week.

I loved the excitement that the world had to offer. But, just at the height of my going out days, God began to tug on my heart. You all remember the days when the party is going good only to have someone come up to you, tap you on your shoulder and say, "Girl, your mom just walked in or your Uncle is here." That puts you in a whole new frame of mind. Just when you are ready to kick it and to take the party to the next level, here comes somebody to ruin the fun.

Well, just at the height of my going out days, at a time I could have really gotten myself into trouble, here comes somebody tapping on my shoulder saying "Girl, God has a greater purpose for your life. This is not who God called you to be and these are not the things that God is calling you to do."

I thought in my mind, "Dang, here we go again. Somebody is always trying to ruin my fun." During the time that God called me, I was grateful for salvation…It's just that I felt like I had a lot of living yet to do. I had a few more good parties left in me.

Another example of God at work in my life is when my husband, Rev. Bailey, accepted his call into the ministry. We had our second son Aaron who had not yet turned one. I was pregnant again but I wasn't showing yet. My sister and some friends of mine were in town. They were talking about hitting the streets. By this time the North End Disco was torn down but there was a spot called the Starlight Terrace that was frequented by all the locals. I was deep in the church by then and really didn't go clubbing but I wanted to go out that night. I wanted just one more time to get dressed up and experience the night life with my sister and girlfriends. I felt as though I was losing myself in this thing called marriage and motherhood. You feel me?

I felt like I had been hoodwinked and bamboozled. Rev. Bailey always said that he felt he was called into the ministry but I honestly thought he meant he was going to announce his call much later in life and

I was all for that. I thought he meant he would go into the ministry when we were in our sixties. That was alright because by then that would give me plenty of time to get all my running out.

Well, back to my story. I didn't know how I was going to broach the subject of me going out with the girls so I waited until the last minute. Richard and Aaron were fed. I cleaned the house from top to bottom and I had secretly gone through several outfits to see what I was going to wear for the night. When the time came for me to get dressed, I decided to "tell" my husband that I was going out for the night. I figured that if I "asked" what he thought then that would give him to room to object.

So, I waited for what I thought was the opportune time for me to spring my news upon him. He got a phone call and was somewhat distracted by being on the phone so I figured this was time to tell him that a few of us girls had decided to go out.

I sprang it on him when he was on the phone. He looked at me, put the person on hold and asked me what in the world I was talking about. Well, Rev. Bailey has pretty much always taken a non-confrontational approach and he said, "well, if that is what you feel you need to do, go ahead and go." He didn't exactly give me his blessing but it was good enough for me. I made a quick switch from housecoat and rollers to being dressed sharp as a tack in less than two and two. I had my hand on the door-knob when I overheard Rev. Bailey say, "No mom, if she wants to go out then who am I to stop her?"

I thought Lord, did he just say "mom?" "Here we go again. Somebody else is trying to ruin my fun." I started to go on out the door. I mean, after all, I was already dressed. My girls were waiting for me. I was home-free. But this still small voice spoke to me once again. *This is not the life I have called you to.* So, I slowly turned around and asked Rev. Bailey what his momma had to say. He quickly tried to shoo me on out the door but I just had to hear what his big-mouth mamma had to say (just kidding Bailey family-they run deep). Not wanting to turn the situation into World War 3, he quickly ended the call and meekly told me what his momma said.

And what had happened was…she apparently told him that I had no business going out to a club since my husband had announced his call into the ministry. But, Rev. Bailey being who he is, encouraged me to go out and have a good time with my friends if that was what I wanted to do.

I was fired up! How dare she imply that I couldn't go out just because he had announced his call into the ministry. I got undressed, got my housecoat back on, washed my face and called my girlfriends and sister to let them know that I couldn't go with them. Rev. Bailey quickly excused himself and went to bed.

I had myself a huge pity party that night. I cried because I was married with children, had to miss yet another party, was tethered at a young age to this preacher and just felt like my life was over. To make matters worse, my girls went on without me! Ain't that some stuff? They could have come over and we could have had ourselves a movie night or something. I got out a bucket and a sponge and mopped my floors on my hands and knees that night all the while crying and saying how life was so unfair to me.

None of these things in and of themselves are wrong. I could have gone to the clubs, hung out, kicked it, etc. Here's the problem. I have what they call an "addictive personality." An addictive personality refers to a particular set of personality traits that make an individual predisposed to developing addictions. This hypothesis states that there are common elements among people with varying addictions that relates to personality traits. I sincerely believe that God placed various roadblocks up throughout my life to protect me from myself. I felt like I was missing out on a whole lot of fun but now I can look back and exclaim, "God blocked it!"

I learned something from what Paul said in Philippians 3. He says, "Yet whatever gains I had, these I have come to regard as loss because of Christ. More than that, I regard everything as loss because of the surpassing value of knowing Christ Jesus my Lord.

For His sake, I have suffered the loss of all things, and I regard them as rubbish, in order that I may gain Christ and be found in Him, not having righteousness of my own that comes from the law, but one that comes through faith in Christ, the righteousness from God based on faith." (Philippians 3:7-9)

22

Double the Blessings!

When our son Aaron was nine months old, I learned I was pregnant again. Way to go Jimmy. You did it again! We discussed having another child but did not plan to so quite so soon. Two months into the pregnancy, I developed complications and was rushed to the hospital fearing I was having a miscarriage. On our way to the hospital, we knew to pray for the best but to be prepared for the worst. The technician performing the ultrasound assured us that not only could one heartbeat be detected but in fact, there were two!

The look on my husband's face was priceless. To say we were surprised was an absolute understatement. We could not believe the news. A few more weeks into the pregnancy, a second ultrasound revealed that both babies were girls. Tears of joy rolled down my face as I thanked God for bringing my family to its perfect completion; two boys and two girls.

I was blessed to carry the twins for thirty-eight weeks. My mother who was living in Chicago at the time traveled to Quincy during the anticipated time of their arrival. She stayed in town for several days anxiously awaiting their arrival. They were on their own timeline however and mom regretfully announced she had to return to Chicago for work the following day. I appreciated the time she was able to spend with us in Quincy but understood she had to return to Chicago. I really did not want to go through this experience without her however and somehow the twins must have sensed it. I went into labor late that evening and was blessed to have both mom and my husband with me as the girls made their way into the world. We named them Ebony and Aliya and like our sons, Richard and Aaron, they have been the center of our world for many years. We love them with all that we are and they have added a richness to our lives that is everlasting.

As wonderful as children are, the transition of going from having one child to four children in a matter of two years was overwhelming. Before I gave birth to the twins, I expressed my concern to my mother in law as I was worried how we were going to handle our ever- growing family. She told me not to worry about a thing because the Lord would provide. She further assured me that she would be there to help myself and Jim in every way possible. My mother in law meant what she said. Both she and God did come through and in a mighty way. She opened her heart by allowing our entire family to move into her home and was there every day, assisting with the feedings, bathing and clothing of the children. Jim was working full-time but God worked it out that I had her there to help the entire time. Only He knew how much I would need it because one of the twins was delivered by natural birth and the other had to be delivered by c-section due to the spirit of rebellion. I'm not going to tell you which twin was the culprit because I don't want to be petty. I will tell you we have since worked through our issues in therapy (lol). In all seriousness, though, I would have been hard pressed to have made it through that through that challenging period of my life without the help of my mother-in-love Mary Bailey. She is a second mother to me and I am forever in her debt for the love she demonstrated towards all of us. Thank you, momma Bailey. I love you.

23

Fast Forward

ife in the social service world eventually began to take a toll on me. After spending close
to twenty years in the field, I began to suffer from what is known as Vicarious Trauma. The
American Counseling Association defines Vicarious
Trauma as the emotional residue of exposure that
counselors have from working with people as they
are hearing their trauma stories and become witnesses to the pain, fear, and terror that trauma survivors
have endured. I reached a point where every story
that I heard attached itself to me like a weight, and

before I knew it, I was sinking further and further into an ocean of sadness. I also suffered from bouts of anxiety. This led to panic attacks—the works. I knew my body was trying to tell me something but I wasn't trying to hear it. So, I carried on the best that I could. I was present at work, but I wasn't really there. I went through the motions of seeing patients but I really wasn't listening. I was really in self-protective mode and doing all I could to tune them out. I had had enough. I simply couldn't carry any more weight.

I was facing a dilemma, a crisis of sorts and I knew I had to make some life changing decisions. "Should I stay or should I go?" I knew I needed to walk away but I was reluctant to do so. I was good at this kind of work. I felt this was my life's calling. This is what I went to school for. I had a good rapport with the patients. I felt they needed me. What would other people think? I had to have a job. Who would I be if I left the field? It was a huge part of my identity. Helping people is simply what I do.

Kenny Rogers coined these infamous lyrics in his

song "The Gambler." "You got to know when to hold 'em, know when to fold 'em, know when to walk away, and know when to run." I could and should have applied this advice as it related to my career but I was bound and determined to hold on. My therapist had long since recommended I resign from my position, but like thousands if not millions of Americans, I kept pushing my body, ignoring the warning signs, denying my body much needed rest until my body began to rebel.

I began suffering panic attacks at work. I have always prided myself on being an excellent employee, maintaining an upbeat cooperative attitude, being a real team player, being someone who was supportive and reliable. That all changed. I started calling in sick and when I did go to work I was "there" physically but no longer on my game. I became irritable and edgy with my coworkers, much less tolerant of others…let's just call it foolishness. I began taking extended lunch hours or leaving early to avoid returning to a place that had grown intolerable.

In the Spring of 2015, as quiet as it was kept, I took a medical leave of absence from my job. I knew that it was time. The stakes had become too high. I feared I would continue to spiral downward causing considerable damage to myself as well as my family. I witnessed it happening to many of my coworkers and I knew it was time for me to step away.

24

Do You Know Where You're Going To? Do You Like the Things That Life is Showing You?

My decision to resign from my job was a matter of self-preservation. Although I longed to remain in the field of social services and to devote my time helping others heal, I was fully aware of the importance of taking care of myself. When flying on a commercial airline, the flight attendants routinely warns, "In case of a loss in cabin pressure, oxygen masks above your seats will deploy. Please place the mask on yourself first and then on your child or other passengers." They admonish you to do so because you cannot help anyone else if you have not adequately taken care of yourself. My own health was in jeopardy and it was time to make some changes.

I have lived with Major Depression for several years, though it's been manageable, my symptoms have worsened in recent years. Depression and other mental health issues are said to be caused by a combination of genetic (inherited) or environmental factors (situations occurring in your environment). I am not a doctor but allow me to elaborate per my level of understanding.

Having a history of mental illness in the family does not automatically result in the development of mental illness in the offspring. Some may never develop mental illness while others may eventually develop symptoms.

As for me, I can trace its symptoms back to my childhood. As I mentioned before, I was a constant behavior problem in school and I suffered from unbelievable anxiety. I didn't know it then but I know exactly what it was now. I was always in motion, always moving, unable to sit still, unable to stop talking, restless, nervous, always uneasy.

As I mentioned earlier in the book, because of the trauma I had lived with in my childhood, the sexual abuse, the undiagnosed depression and anxiety, I did attempt to end my life at the age of eleven years old. As I look back now, I realize that I didn't really want to die, I just no longer wanted to live in that constant state of confusion and sadness. I desperately wanted to be happy, to be normal like the other kids around me. I wanted to be able to genuinely smile and to enjoy life. Instead I felt as if I were dying a slow death and there was no one around to help me. Keeping secrets kill but somehow, I survived.

My official diagnosis of Major Depression would not come until after the birth of our second child. I began to suspect I was suffering from symptoms of Post-Partum Depression. Post-Partum Depression could last from a period of a few weeks to a year after delivery. It is most common in the first three months. Problem is, my depression did not go away. Although I worked hard to present a brave front, I suffered from bouts of uncontrollable crying. Finding the energy to get out of bed in the morning was a major feat. I could not muster up the energy to get up and get myself dressed. I knew I could not go on living that way. It was then that I decided to seek help. I made an appointment with my family doctor and was prescribed an anti-depressant. I also begin seeing a therapist to address the trauma I had sustained in my youth and both helped to alleviate my symptoms of depression.

Eventually I was weaned off the medication as I was hoping that the depression would be manageable through therapy alone. I experienced a recurrence of symptoms and reluctantly agreed to resume the medication.

Acceptance of a diagnosis of Major Depression was difficult. I felt like a failure. I had been through and sustained so much so why couldn't I just shake this thing? Why couldn't I control it, suck it up, get it together, and just move on? Where was my faith? Where was my God?

But eventually I grew tired of being sick and tired. I was sick of hurting, sick of making poor decisions. I was sick of self-sabotage, sick of repeating the same poor patterns of behavior, sick of "stinking thinking" so I decided to take control of my health and fight back!

I worked with my doctor to develop a plan of treatment that works for me and has gotten me back on the road to recovery.

I have learned to take each day one day at a time. I start out my day with prayer and devotion to God. I make a list of things that I am grateful for so that I can channel my mind and thoughts in the right direction. Clinical Depression is much more than just feeling sad or just a case of the blues. It unfortunately affects many areas of your life. The self-defeating voices and thoughts don't stop so I actively work to feed my mind with thoughts of hope, faith, and promise.

Depression is like a CD that constantly plays in my mind. Depression or depressive thoughts come with their own message. These thoughts tell me that I am a failure, that I am unlovable, inadequate and incapable of succeeding.

In my recovery, I must choose to take active steps on a daily basis to change the CD that is playing in my mind. This takes an amazing amount of energy and one misstep can throw me off my game. The rewards are worth it however because the new CD reminds me that I am wonderfully blessed, that I am strong, that I am loved and that I can make a difference in this world. If I don't do this on a daily basis, the depressive mind naturally defaults to the depressive CD. It is up to me to change it!

Another thing I do to stay on my game is to exercise which I do five to six days a week. I usually give myself at least one day off for good behavior. Science proves that exercise releases endorphins in the brain which are responsible for naturally making us feel good. I am all for anything that will make me feel good, that is legal and comes with zero guilt. Exercise makes me feel so much better about myself, gives me time and space to plan and "own" my day and is a great stress reliever.

The third thing I try to do is to watch what I eat. I cannot expect to function well if I continuously poison my body. There's a clear relationship between food and your state of mind. I know that sugar is not good for me. It may spike my mood temporarily but I soon begin to feel terribly sluggish. I don't need that because Depression does a pretty good job of that on its own! Why add to an already existing problem? Plus, I have issues with food; the cleaner I eat, the better I feel about myself. So, I try to eat a healthy diet while recognizing I only live once. I don't want to eat salads everyday so I try to practice the 80/20 rule, 80% clean, 20% wiggle room. It's a compromise I can live with.

Additionally, sleep is very important so I try to maintain a consistent bedtime each night. Sometimes that means saying no to certain activities but I have realized how important it is to get adequate rest. Becoming overly tired has been the cause of many depressive episodes and I work to try to prevent them as much as possible.

While I am on the topic, let me clue you in on an acronym that you may or may not be aware of (H.A.L.T.) This stands for Hungry, Angry, Lonely, Tired. It is important that you are aware of your levels in all four of these areas because they have often led well-meaning people to make poor decisions. I try not to run too low in any of these four domains because that is when I venture into the land of "stinking thinking," which again is making decisions that I may not ordinarily make if I my thinking tank was on FULL.

I live with Asthma and have since I was two years old. My asthma is often exercise induced so although I still engage in exercise, I have learned to modify certain exercises to prevent an asthma attack. I have learned to manage my symptoms by carefully listening to my body and when I experience problems, I schedule an appointment with my doctor and she prescribes a course of treatment that will once again stabilize my breathing. My asthma is a problem that affects my lungs but it has not stopped me from living a productive life.

Depression is a disease that has affected my brain. I have heard people ask, "what is it that you have to be depressed about? Or "How can you be depressed?" That is the equivalent of saying, "How could you have asthma?" or "How could you have diabetes?" It is a disease. Asthma is a disease that affects my lungs, Depression is a disease that affects my brain, plain and simple! No one that I know wants to have Asthma and no one that I know wants to have Depression but neither condition has to be a death sentence and neither condition is anyone's fault. They are both medical conditions. With a commitment to a plan of wellness, a solid system of support (which may or may not include family), I believe recovery is attainable for everyone.

I share this information so that others will know

that they are not alone, they are not powerless and that individuals who live with mental illness can and do live happy, productive lives. I'm living proof.

25

Come Out, Come Out, Wherever You Are!

A few years ago, someone that I love dearly suffered a death in their family as the result of suicide. This death affected me greatly as the individual was a member of the body of Christ. This person knew the Lord and attended church on a regular basis but yet suffered from such deep personal pain and anguish that suicide appeared to be their only option.

Suicide is not anyone's fault. It is a decision that the individual has chosen to make when they feel they can no longer bear the pain of living this life. There may or may not be symptoms indicating an individual is in distress. Oftentimes those who suffer mental health symptoms are reluctant to seek help. In many cases, untreated mental health disorders can result in suicidal thoughts or gestures. My heart truly grieves for those who are left to mourn their loved one's passing. I pray God's peace and comfort for all who suffer this dreaded disease.

I took this young man's death personally because I too have been at that point of desperation in my life; smiling on the outside yet suffering greatly on the inside. I too am a member of the body of Christ. I attend church on a regular basis. I pray, fast, tithe, believe His word, take Him at His word and yet, I live with Major Depression. I have lived with it for over 20 years. Despite my best effort, *sometimes* the pain simply doesn't go away. There are times when I can't pray it away, I can't fast it away, I can't rebuke it away. Trust me, I've tried. Like the Apostle Paul, I asked the Lord thrice (at least) to take this condition away from me. He responded, "my grace is sufficient for you."

I never spoke of my condition because of stigma and shame. However, when this intelligent, beautiful, charismatic person died, I made the decision to remove my masks and admit that I too hurt, so that those who struggled would know that they are not alone. I made a promise that his death would not be in vain. I decided then to take up the mantle and join in the fight against the stigma related to mental illness.

God has blessed me. He continues to strengthen me. I am not hopeless. I am not powerless. I am a victor, not a victim. I know that all things work together for my good. I have been called to spread the "good news" that we who live with mental health issues are no different than those of us who live with physical illness. God loves YOU. YOU are not damaged. YOU are needed in the kingdom of God. There is room for you at the cross.

26

I Survived Ministries...

had come to terms with the reality that I was living with a mental health condition, was going to all my doctor's appointments, taking my meds like a good girl, attending a few low-key mental health meetings...there you go! I fulfilled my mental health advocacy obligations. So why won't the Lord leave me alone? Why is He always asking for more, more, more! I found my answer to the question in the scriptures. The word of God says, "To whom much is given, much will be required. (Luke 12:48)

I felt the Lord calling me to do more. I didn't

quite know what "more" was but I continued to have a strong stirring in my spirit and all I could do was to wait on Him to speak. I had long since given the Lord permission to use me but I had some stipulations. Imagine having ten different doors to your life. I had given God access to eight of them, allowing Him to use any of the eight for His glory. Two of those doors however were "off limits" because they contained things too ugly, too painful to be of any benefit. Those doors had been sealed off from public viewing. That concept shouldn't be too foreign to God because didn't He do the same thing in the Garden of Eden. He said, "You could eat of any trees in the garden except for this one right here…" Well I thought I would try the same method but it didn't work. God wanted to open the very doors that I had marked "off limits". He wanted to use those doors for His glory!

When I finally told the Lord "Yes," He gave me the name of this ministry, "I Survived". What this means to me is that yes, I have dealt with many difficulties in life, but I Survived and I will go on to achieve great things in Jesus name. The scriptural basis is 2 Corinthians 4:8-9 "We are hard pressed on every side, but not crushed; perplexed, but not in despair; persecuted, but not abandoned; struck down, but not destroyed."

Here I would be remiss if I did not give a special acknowledgment to someone I call one of my best friends but who is more like a sister to me—Consuelo Ross. She and I have been sister friends for over thirty years. They used to refer to us as Salt-N-Pepa because we were as thick as thieves back in the day and we still are. As close as we are, there are so many things I have never told her, so many things I kept bottled up inside of me. When I began to share with her, she was absolutely astounded, but to her credit, she rolled with the punches and supported me whole-heartedly. She will never, ever know how vital and meaningful her response was.

Consuelo responded with empathy and support. She jumped on board and donated countless hours to support the I Survived mission. She along with my daughter Aliya, who designed the I Survived t-shirt as well as helped develop the website, worked diligently to make the vision a reality. Their compassion, love, and belief in me served as the energy I needed to get I Survived off the ground. I am eternally grateful.

God has opened doors that no man can shut. I am privileged to share my story of recovery in the Chicago Public School system as a Lead Presenter through partnership with the National Alliance on Mental Illness (NAMI), serving as a panelist for the Cook County Sheriff's Department and the Chicago Police Department's Crisis Intervention Team (CIT) training program, and sharing in local hospitals and outpatient settings. My story is two-fold. It touches on topics such as domestic violence, childhood sexual abuse, homelessness, but it also highlights components of my recovery: my faith, proper nutrition, daily exercise, importance of getting adequate sleep, medication, and yes letting everyone know that in spite of it all, I survived!

I Survived will partner with existing agencies to reduce the stigma related to mental illness, participate in public education forums and health fairs, educate and inform others of the importance of managing their mental health. I Survived will assist churches as they seek ways to minister to congregants who are living with mental health issues.

I Survived to let others know that they too can survive. God is leading me to spread this message everywhere I go: schools, churches, hospitals, prisons. I survived and so can you. I am a witness. What He has done for me, He can and will do for you.

It is my hope that others will join in the I Survived movement and find courage to share their stories of recovery whether it involves mental illness, substance abuse, physical or sexual abuse, grief, cancer or other physical challenges. I do believe the scriptures where it says we overcome by the blood of the lamb and by the word of our testimony (Revelation 12:11).

We all have a story to share. God has moved mightily in all our lives and we should not be ashamed to tell of the good news of Jesus for it is the power of God that brings salvation. Each of us has been commissioned to go ye into all the world and to preach the gospel into every nation and I fully believe by sharing your 'I Survived' testimony, by sharing your scars, sharing your experiences, sharing what God has truly brought you through and delivered you from, others might want to know this awesome God for themselves. Everybody ought to know WHO Jesus is. Don't you agree? I Survived and so did you! So, Go, tell it on the mountain, over the hills and everywhere! Go and tell how God has made a real difference in your life and how He can make a difference in the lives of others if they would invite Him in. He did it for me. He will do the same for you!

My name is Ericka Bailey and **#I Survived**.

Epilogue

I am fully aware that some the content of this book may have been unsettling if not disturbing. If you found it too much to read, imagine the horrors of living through it. I wrote the book as my declaration of independence. I wrote it for the purpose of letting others who may have faced similar circumstances know that though they have been through hell, they too can survive! I wrote it to end the silence of abuse and empower others to find their voice and to find the courage to take back their lives.

Chicago held terrible memories for me and when I moved away in 1986, I had no intention of ever returning. It is said that time heals all wounds, and while my wounds were not healed, in time I did find the courage to return for the occasional visit. My mother and sister still lived in Chicago. My father lived there as well. This may be hard for some to understand (it's even harder for me to write) but I loved my father and I chose to forgive him for what he had done. He owned up to it. He asked me how it was that I could forgive him and still love him when he and I both knew what he tried to do to me. My answer to him was "because you're my dad and I love you." I was willing to forgive him in order to have him as a part of my life. When he passed away in 1991, it was I who sang a song of tribute at his funeral. Again, I have found it is completely possible to love the person while hating the harmful things they have done to you.

My husband is a Pastor in the A.M.E. Church and we are subject to being moved at the discretion of our Bishop. Our lives in the ministry is similar to the military. In the A.M.E. church, moving is merely a part of the process. In 2011 we were assigned to a church on the West Side of Chicago in the middle of our conference year. We had to move and move quickly. Gone were the quick two to three day trips, this time we were expected to take up residency. I was to come face to face with a city that had haunted me for many years and I had a husband and children there as witnesses.

We moved to the side of town that I knew best— the North side and enrolled the kids in the same high school I had attended before moving back to Quincy. Unbeknownst to them, being in that particular area, though familiar was difficult for me as most of my time up North had been spent with Mister. I could not afford to look elsewhere because I did not want my children missing out on school. They were already being uprooted mid-semester.

I had come to a fork in the road. I could continue to be held captive by painful memories or I could choose to do something about it. I chose the latter of the two options and deliberately set out to visit various locations on the North side where painful memories existed so that I could go, face them and create a different set of memories. For example, I remember where I was the first time I had been slapped by Mister. I went to that same location, faced it, recognized I was no longer that person and no longer in that situation, thereby releasing its hold on me.

Determined to be free from the ghosts of my past, I traveled to as many locations as I could remember, by bike or by car. I went to the apartment Mister and I shared where I was the target of his abuse, went to his aunt's house, went to my former middle school, went by friends' apartments where we used to hang out, went to that cemetery where I had to run for my life to escape the abductor we tried to rob, went by my mother's apartment where the stalking occurred, went by the apartment where he chased me up the stairs and pulled me back down ripping the skin off of my back, on and on I went until I neutralized each and every area, thereby releasing its hold on me. I was determined to not be held captive by ugly memories. I was determined to be free!

This exercise proved to be very beneficial as I was required to revisit many of those areas during our four year stay on the North side. We have since moved out of the city and to the Western Suburbs.

As I mentioned earlier in the book, I heard from Mister sporadically throughout the years. His phone calls were always filled with promises of checks and clothing that had been sent for our son but would somehow mysteriously get lost in the mail. They were either never sent or the postmaster's son was masterfully dressed; I'm not sure which one was which. He and I would not meet face to face until 2015, almost 30 years later. I received word that his brother had died and I made the decision to attend the funeral. I chose to go for several reasons. My husband Jimmy had been in Richard's life since Richard was two and was a wonderful father to him. He was the only father Richard had known. Richard and I had had some discussions about his biological father. I provided very brief information throughout the years because I wanted to protect him until Richard was an adult and able to protect himself. Richard had questions about his paternal side of the family and rightly so. I felt the time had come to bridge the gap and allow Richard the opportunity to connect should he choose to do so in the future, and I knew that I had the power to make that connection happen for him. He did ultimately connect with his biological father and met him face to face. I was not present for that meeting and I will not go into details because that is Richard's story to tell.

The second reason I attended the funeral was to express my condolences to Mister's mother as well to show her the respect I should have shown her years ago. We were young, selfish, and reckless but that gave us no right to disrespect her house or her rules and I wanted to accept responsibility for my actions. It was nice to talk, laugh, cry and even pray together on that day.

Lastly, I went to the funeral as a way of closure. I wanted and needed to close out the chapter with Mister in my life. I did it as a way to come full-circle. I had done a lot of work in therapy and on my own to exorcise the demons that had been plaguing me, and in terms of my life with him, this was it. I was able to look at him directly in his eyes, after years of nightmares, after years of looking over my shoulders, after years of self-destructive behavior, I had come to let him know, I may have some scars, but I Survived!

Jimmy and I have celebrated our 27th wedding anniversary. We are empty-nesters now, which is quite different but exciting at the same time. We have a four-year old grandson named Atticus James Monroe by our oldest son Richard. His is a delightful little boy! There is a scripture in the Bible Joel 2:25, "I will repay you for the years the locusts have eaten." I have found that scripture to be true. God has blessed us with so much, more than what we could ever ask or think and I am very grateful.

My mother is doing well and I believe she is proud of the woman I have become. She is a private woman so I thank her for allowing me to be used by God in a way that is bigger than all of us. My mother is a God-fearing woman and believes in walking in obedience to His will. She is a survivor in her own right and has taught me to stand strong and to fight. I love that little lady with my whole heart and would give my very last to see a smile on her face.

Momma, "You are once, twice, three times a lady, and I love you!" I dedicate this book to you...I Survived!!!

65648253R00094

Made in the USA
Lexington, KY
19 July 2017